RUNNER'S WORLD® GUIDE TO

CROSS-TRAINING

MATT FITZGERALD

RODALE

Runner's World is a registered trademark of Rodale Inc.

Printed in the United States of America
Rodale Inc. makes every effort to use acid-free ∞, recycled paper ♻ .

The Healthy Eating Pyramid on page 207 is reprinted with the permission of Simon &
Schuster Source, from *Eat, Drink and Be Healthy* by Dr. Walter C. Willett, © 2001
President and Fellows of Harvard College

Book design by Drew Frantzen

Library of Congress Cataloging-in-Publication Data
Fitzgerald, Matt.
    Runner's world guide to cross-training / Matt Fitzgerald.
        p.   cm.
    Includes index.
    ISBN 1—57954—783—4 paperback
    1. Running—Training.   2. Exercise.   3. Physical fitness.   I. Title: Guide to cross-
training.   II. Runner's world.   III. Title.
GV1061.5.F58   2004
613.7'11—dc22   2004011268

Distributed to the trade by Holtzbrinck Publishers

2   4   6   8   10   9   7   5   3   1   paperback

RODALE

WE **INSPIRE** AND **ENABLE** PEOPLE TO IMPROVE
THEIR LIVES AND THE WORLD AROUND THEM

FOR MORE OF OUR PRODUCTS
WWW.RODALESTORE.COM
(800) 848-4735

CONTENTS

ACKNOWLEDGMENTS

I would like to express my deepest thanks to the many runners, coaches, and others whose various contributions made this book possible and better: Richard Benyo, Amby Burfoot, Leah Flickinger, Josh Fitzgerald, Jeff Galloway, Christina Gandolfo, Dan Gilbert, Joe Henderson, Libbie Hickman, Deena Kastor, Jeremy Katz, Meb Keflezighi, Khalid Khannouchi, David Krummenacker, Kathryn LeSage, Bob Larsen, Cathy O'Brien, Andrea Pedolsky, Steve Plasencia, Robert Portman, Dathan Ritzenhein, Lou Schuler, Ryan Shay, and Joe Vigil.

INTRODUCTION

This book grew out of my own experience as an athlete. I had been running competitively for 15 years when I got a notion to branch into triathlons. In doing so, I expected that my running background would give me a solid foundation for progress in swimming and cycling, and this proved to be the case. But to my astonishment, I also found that multidisciplinary training made me a better runner. I gained speed, efficiency, and endurance on foot despite the fact that I was running less, and I also suffered fewer injuries and experienced greater overall motivation for training.

After making this happy discovery, I began to experiment with various ways of using cross-training to enhance my running apart from my interest in triathlons. Experimentation was indeed necessary, because my search for solid cross-training principles and methods among the established running experts turned up surprisingly little. Through trial and error, I was able to collect a reliable set of methods, which I then began prescribing to the runners I coached, who achieved similar benefits. The next step was to take my cross-training approach to the broader community of runners.

By no means is the guidance in this book based solely on my experience as a runner and coach, however. I didn't invent flexibility training, strength training, or any of the forms of nonimpact endurance training discussed in the following pages. Nor did I create any of the established principles and methods of training for distance-running events. All I've done is find some reliable ways of putting together running and these complementary forms of training. And I'm not the only person to have done even this much. In writing this book, I benefited from the input of other coaches and elite runners who represent the vanguard of the cross-training approach to competitive running.

The basic philosophy that these runners and coaches share with me is simple: Runners cannot succeed by only running. If you want to be as healthy, fit, and fulfilled as you can be as a runner, your training should involve not only running but also flexibility training, strength training, and one or more forms of nonimpact endurance training, such as bicycling or deep-water running. In a word (or, technically, four words), you need to cross-train.

Most runners have a basic understanding that they should cross-train, yet they nevertheless tend to cross-train erratically, unsystematically, and without clear purpose, if at all. The problem is not in the runners themselves; it is in the resources runners rely on for training information and guidance. The coaches and running experts from whom runners learn how to train, directly and indirectly, have tended not to make a strong enough case for cross-training and have treated it as a peripheral rather than central component of training. Worse, they often contradict one another in the cross-training recommendations they give.

What runners need in order to cross-train effectively is a complete and authoritative guide to cross-training. That is what I have set out to provide in this book. My aim is to give you all of the motivation, information, and perspective you need to cross-train for success in running, whether success for you means finishing a 10-K or winning a marathon.

There is no single right way to cross-train for running. As with your running itself, how *you* should cross-train depends on several factors, including your goals, personal preferences, and past and present injuries, as well as how your body responds to various types of training. Nevertheless, every runner needs to cross-train consistently, systematically, and purposefully, using proven methods that apply universally to all runners. The first step is to fundamentally change the way you view your training. Stop seeing cross-training modalities as the icing on the cake of training. Start viewing them as the very meat of training, along with running itself. How do you make this shift? It happens quite naturally when you get a clear understanding of the full range of benefits of cross-training (which happens to be the subject of chapter 1). The next step is to give proper cross-training a legitimate try. Once you have experienced the benefits for yourself, there's no turning back. That's how we runners work.

Warmed up? Good. Let's make strides.

ONE

EIGHT BENEFITS OF CROSS-TRAINING

IF YOU ASK 10 OTHER RUNNERS to name a benefit of cross-training, at least 8 of them will mention injury prevention. But although injury prevention is by far the most widely recognized benefit of cross-training among runners, it's hardly the only one. Runners can also use cross-training to rehabilitate injuries, improve fitness, promote recovery, enhance motivation, rejuvenate the mind and body during breaks from formal training, enjoy competing in other endurance sports, and even stay fit through pregnancy. Related to the benefit of injury prevention, cross-training can also prolong your running career.

The good news is that you don't have to do eight different kinds of cross-training to get these eight distinct benefits (seven if you're male). You can enjoy them all by supplementing your running with a little strength training, flexibility training, and endurance cross-training (for instance, bicycling or swimming). Each of these three forms of cross-training has its own relationship to the benefits I've just mentioned, but there's plenty of overlap.

Strength training is most useful for injury prevention and rehabilitation and improving running fitness. Flexibility training helps primarily with injury prevention and rehabilitation and recovery. Alternative forms of cardiovascular conditioning are useful in relation to all eight benefits, although much depends on the specific form of exercise. For example, bicycling is generally more useful than swimming as a means of improving running fitness, since it increases leg strength. But it may be less useful than swimming for certain cases of injury rehabilitation.

As you get deeper into the book, I'll say more about the specific effects of these three forms of cross-training and show you how to incorporate each into your overall training program. Here, I'll simply sell you on the benefits. We runners aren't lazy, but we are practical. Once we believe something will improve our running, we'll make the effort to include it in our programs. Until then, we won't. We can't afford to waste our time and energy on workouts that are more hype than help. Here's my case.

BENEFIT #1: INJURY PREVENTION

Overuse injuries are the curse of the running life, a never-ending epidemic among pavement (and trail) pounders everywhere. Studies suggest that as many as 50 percent of competitive runners miss at least a few days of training each year because of injuries, and most of those injuries are from the chronic grind of training. (Acute injuries, from slips and stumbles, are much less common.) Indeed, you'd be hard-pressed to find a runner of more than a few years' experience who hasn't come up lame with shin splints, runner's knee, plantar fasciitis, Achilles tendinitis, or another common running-related overuse condition. If I were a betting man, I'd wager you have had at least one of these injuries at least once.

Nevertheless, injuries aren't inevitable. Most overuse injuries can be prevented or at least prevented from returning. (More than half of running injuries are actually reinjuries.) Most of them can be blamed on four factors.

1. **Inadequate recovery (when your body doesn't fully recover from one run to the next)**

2. **Biomechanical irregularities (such as overpronation and leg-length discrepancy)**

3. **Muscular imbalances caused by running itself (tight hamstrings and weak quadriceps, for example)**

4. **Improper or worn-out footwear**

Cross-training can't help you with your footwear choices, but it can address the other three factors.

THE BENEFITS OF CROSS-TRAINING FOR RUNNING PERFORMANCE

The table below shows how a well-rounded cross-training program results in better overall preparation for running competition. The first column lists 10 attributes that runners seek to increase through training. The second column indicates the effect that proper run training will likely have on each of these attributes. An upward arrow indicates enhancement, a downward arrow indicates diminishment, and a pair of arrows indicates a mixed effect or an effect that depends on circumstances. The three columns to the right indicate the effect that each of the three types of cross-training will likely have on each of the 10 attributes when combined with a good run-training regimen.

	RUNNING ONLY	ENDURANCE CROSS-TRAINING	STRENGTH TRAINING	FLEXIBILITY TRAINING
Endurance	↑	↑		
Efficiency	↑	↑	↑	↑
Speed	↑	↑		
Power	↑	↑	↑	
Dynamic Flexibility	↑↓[1]	↑↓[1]	↑	↑
Strength	↑	↑	↑	
Joint Stability	↓	↑	↑	↑
Muscle Balance	↓	↑	↑	↑
Motivation	↑↓[2]	↑↓[2]	↑↓[2]	↑↓[2]
Recovery	↑↓	↑	↑	

[1] Running can increase dynamic flexibility in those who start with little, but generally speaking, running itself is not a very effective way to enhance this attribute as compared with strength and flexibility training. Most other endurance disciplines are similar to running in this regard, although each enhances or limits dynamic flexibility in its own way.

[2] Motivation is a highly individual matter. Clearly, if you love running, it will usually motivate you, whereas if you dislike cross-training, it will usually sap your motivation. In my experience, however, the addition of cross-training usually enhances a runner's overall motivation by reducing the monotony of training.

RECOVERY. The term *overuse injury* captures the relationship between recovery and injury prevention. Each workout produces minor injuries within your muscles and connective tissues. Give your body enough time, and it'll not only repair the damage but also make those tissues stronger and more durable in order to prevent future damage. This is why virtually every book about running tells you to increase your training workload carefully and gradually and to avoid hard workouts when you're sore or fatigued.

Still, experienced runners inevitably reach a point at which they can't improve their already high fitness levels without risking an overuse injury. Yet if they stay within their ability to recover from workouts, they won't improve.

This is where cross-training can be helpful. By supplementing your running with endurance-improving exercises that are easy on your joints—such as water running and bicycling—you can lower the risk of overuse injuries without forsaking fitness.

BIOMECHANICAL IRREGULARITIES. Deviations from correct stride mechanics contribute to most injuries. The most common culprit is overpronation (excessive inward rolling of the foot), which is believed to contribute to more than half of all running injuries. Cross-training activities such as inline skating and strength exercises requiring balance can reduce overpronation by improving ankle strength and proprioception (the ability of the muscles and tendons to feed the brain information about their positioning).

MUSCULAR IMBALANCES. Usually, a muscle group that does a lot of work in running becomes tight while an opposing muscle group becomes correspondingly weak; as a result, the tightened muscle may tear, or an affected joint may become unstable and eventually damaged. For example, weakness in the hip muscles can cause a runner's leg to rotate inward on impact, causing overpronation of the foot, which might in turn cause Achilles tendinitis. By this example, you can see that muscular imbalances and form problems are closely related. Most cases of muscular imbalance contribute to form problems, and form problems tend to exacerbate muscular imbalances.

So if muscles are weaker or tighter than they should be, it makes intuitive sense that strength and flexibility training will fix the problem. It's also logical that preemptive strengthening and stretching can head off typical running injuries.

If you're a beginning runner who hasn't yet developed strength and flexibility imbalances, you can get big benefits from endurance cross-training. Your ankles, knees, and lower back aren't used to the repetitive impact of running, so you can use walking, elliptical machines, and other low-impact conditioning tools to improve endurance without beating up your most vulnerable joints, muscles, and connective tissues. You can gradually mix in some running once you've established a base of fitness (and lost some weight, if that's an issue).

Endurance cross-training can therefore help you ease into the sport, if you're a new runner, by reducing the amount of impact your body absorbs. And if you're a veteran runner, it helps you stay in the sport. It isn't uncommon for longtime runners to lose so much knee cartilage through repetitive impact that they develop osteoarthritis and are forced to hang up their shoes. By mixing in some weight lifting and swimming today, you just might spare yourself the frustration of *only* being able to swim and lift weights in the future.

BENEFIT #2: REHABILITATION

When an overuse injury does develop, cross-training comes to the rescue in two ways: by helping runners maintain fitness despite being forced to run less or not at all and by correcting the cause of the injury.

Anytime you notice a running-related pain anywhere in your body, the first thing you should do is modify your training to avoid exacerbating the problem. In many cases, this will require that you abort your current workout. Quitting a run can be psychologically painful, but not as painful as the injury is likely to become if you keep going. I recall feeling the first twinge of a developing shin splint about 3 miles into a scheduled 8-miler. Stubborn guy that I am, I kept running, and of course the pain only increased. I wound up walking the last 2 miles, and I couldn't run again for 2 weeks. A year later, I felt the same twinge, but this time I stopped running when I realized what it was. I took the next day off, then switched to a soft surface (the beach) for my next few workouts, and that was the full extent to which my training was interrupted. Lesson learned.

A fitness-salvaging cross-training plan can greatly reduce the disappointment of having to abandon a run. Simply replace today's planned workout with a similar workout that you can perform pain-free.

When you complete this workout, your next order of business is to reduce the swelling in the area where you're experiencing pain. Swelling

KHALID KHANNOUCHI

Moroccan-born Khalid Khannouchi, who became a U.S. citizen in 2000, has twice set the world record in the marathon. He first set the mark at the 1999 Chicago Marathon, running 2:05:42. Three years later, he shaved 4 seconds off his mark in winning the 2002 London Marathon.

But between these spectacular highs, Khannouchi experienced terrible lows in the form of a series of injuries that led to subpar performances and many scotched racing plans. He developed hamstring strains during the 2000 London Marathon, finished a disappointing third, and was subsequently unable to compete in the U.S. Olympic Trials Marathon. (Khannouchi had struggled mightily to receive U.S. citizenship in time to represent his adopted homeland in the 2000 Olympics in Sydney.)  Other injuries, including back spasms and groin and knee problems, all but wiped out his 2000 and 2001 competitive seasons. Khannouchi made every effort to heal his injuries—especially his troublesome hamstrings—through all the traditional therapies, including friction massage, ultrasound, and heat treatments. But while these remedies promoted recovery, they didn't appear to address the root causes of the injuries and therefore prevent recurrence when he resumed his normal training.

Salvation came with his introduction to Jim and Phil Wharton, a father-and-son team of athlete repairmen based in New York City and leading practitioners of a form of flexibility training called active-isolated, or AI, stretching (which you'll learn more about in chapter 3). AI stretching brought immediate results, correcting Khannouchi's muscular imbalances and lengthening his stride back to road-gobbling proportions from the shuffle it had become.

Khannouchi fell into a routine of one weekly session with the Whartons plus a second performed on his own. His injuries disappeared, he felt great, and his form returned. The first competitive season to follow his adopting this routine was the best of his career.

is a symptom of all overuse injuries, since your body sends blood to the site of an injury to accelerate tissue repair. In most cases, the inflammation, not the tissue damage itself, is the primary cause of the pain you feel. Use ice and anti-inflammatory medications such as ibuprofen to reduce the swelling.

Of course, your immediate goal with any injury is to resume normal training as soon as possible. But if you can't resume normal training immediately, your best option is to adopt a modified training program that allows you to maintain running-specific fitness without exacerbating your injury or prolonging the recovery process. The best alternatives are water running, elliptical training, bicycling, and inline skating, because they closely simulate the action and demands of running. If you can approximate the volume and perhaps the intensity of your running workouts, you should be able to maintain your conditioning. If you've been laid up for a while and you sense that your running fitness is in rapid decline, these cross-training activities should at the very least begin to reverse that process.

In addition, there's the peace of mind you get from knowing you aren't losing your hard-earned fitness. That means you'll be less likely to push your injured self to get back on the road too soon and more likely to be fully healed by the time you do return. If you're vigilant about modifying your training in this way as soon as you realize you're injured, you'll seldom have to miss more than a few days of running at a time.

Your ultimate goal is not just to make your injuries go away but also to prevent their return. That means you must address their causes. As I mentioned above, a muscular imbalance of some kind is involved in most overuse injuries. The best way to identify the specific imbalance or group of imbalances that led to your injury is to visit a professional physical therapist who specializes in working with runners. The therapist will examine the injured area, assess the strength and flexibility of various muscle groups, and observe your running stride. From that information, he or she should be able to tell you what needs fixing.

A second option is to try to isolate the cause on your own. Naturally, you can't hope to trace an injury to its origin as reliably as an experienced physical therapist can. However, most running injuries are so common that you can easily diagnose yours when armed with a description of its symptoms, and the most common causes of each type of injury are well-known, so very often learning the cause of an injury is as simple as learning the name. The final step is learning which stretches and strengthening exercises do the best job of correcting the imbalance in question. In chapter 8, I'll discuss the symptoms and causes of nine common running injuries and how to treat each of them.

While certainly preferable, it isn't always necessary to discover the precise cause of an overuse injury in order to heal it and prevent its return. This is because all runners tend to develop the same muscular imbalances. So if you respond to any overuse injury by allowing it to heal and by initiating and maintaining a stretching and strengthening program designed to address all of the muscular imbalances caused by running, you could very well banish your breakdown forevermore without bothering to learn its name. But why stop there? If you do a comprehensive stretching and strengthening program regardless of your injury status, rather than waiting until you're hurt or focusing on the sites of previous injuries, you should be able to prevent the entire spectrum of common training injuries.

BENEFIT #3: GREATER RUNNING FITNESS

The desire to run faster is universal in running. It's what a philosopher might call the organizing principle of the sport. The object of any race is to cover the designated distance in the least amount of time. A road race without a clock is like a basketball game without a scoreboard. The important difference is that a scoreboard forces a pair of opponents to compete strictly against each other, determining one winner and one loser. A stopwatch allows every runner to compete against him- or herself and to win on one's own terms.

Prior to one race, Olympian and 2:11 marathoner Rod DeHaven was asked if he had a goal. He answered that, sure, he had a goal: He wanted to set a PR, just like everyone else.

There are many worthy motivations to run, but the desire to run faster is the most fundamental. Even if you're slower than most runners and you don't get too caught up in your race times, you still pay attention to them, and establishing a new personal best still gives you satisfaction.

Cross-training is a very reliable means to become a faster runner. To make an absolute statement might be going too far, but I think it's safe to say that *almost* every runner can run faster by cross-training appropriately than by running only. There are three main ways in which sup-

In addition to being one of the greatest American-born marathoners of all time, Joan Benoit (now Joan Samuelson) is also the author of the most celebrated episode of cross-training ever done by a runner.

In 1984, at age 26, Benoit had already broken the American marathon record twice and the world record once. But while preparing for the U.S. Olympic Trials Marathon that would serve as a qualifier for the very first women's Olympic marathon in Los Angeles, she developed a serious knee injury. She tried to train through it, but couldn't.

On April 25, just 17 days before the trials, she was forced to have arthroscopic surgery.

No sooner had the general anesthetic worn off than Benoit began stationary cycling and swimming in a desperate attempt to maintain her fitness level and restore full functionality to her knee. She was able to complete only a handful of short runs before the trials, but on her day of reckoning, the knee held up for the full 26.2 miles, and she won the race handily.

As you probably know, Benoit also went on to win the Olympic marathon later that summer with a commanding performance. (She also won the 10,000 meters, which was only an exhibition competition and not yet a medal event in that olympiad.) The following year, she set yet another American record in the marathon (2:21:21) that stood until 2003. She continued to run at a high level for many years, finishing ninth in the 2000 Olympic Trials Marathon at age 42. But she will always be best remembered for her gold-medal run in Los Angeles, which would never have happened if she hadn't used cross-training so effectively to rehabilitate her surgically repaired knee.

plemental training outside the discipline of running can enhance one's running ability. Specifically, it can:

1. **Enhance a runner's efficiency**

2. **Increase a runner's power**

3. **Increase the amount of time a runner is able to spend training without accumulating fatigue or getting injured**

Efficiency is the rate at which a runner burns energy while maintaining a given pace. It's hugely important in long-distance running, because running out of energy is one of the primary limiters of endurance performance. Most runners can maintain world-class marathon pace for a short distance—between 40 yards and a few miles. In other words, the speed is no big deal. But what makes world-class marathoners special is that they burn so little energy while running at this pace that they can hold it for a full 26 miles and 385 yards.

One way cross-training can increase efficiency is by increasing the amount of muscle tissue that can participate in the running action. By mixing your run training with supplemental training in modalities that are similar to running, you "rewire" your body's neuromuscular patterns for running so that they involve more motor units. (A motor unit is a single nerve cell and all the muscle fibers it activates, which can range from one fiber to thousands.) This has the immediate effect of spreading the workload more broadly and thereby decreasing the rate at which energy supplies are depleted from each motor unit. Consider—to cite a morbid example—how much farther eight pallbearers might carry a casket than four. In addition, there's a long-term conditioning effect. The "new" muscle fibers you train in other endurance disciplines undergo the same kinds of changes that running has already produced in other muscle fibers—increases in aerobic enzymes, capillary density, and so forth. This makes them capable of better endurance performance.

Cross-training can also increase your running efficiency by eliminating wasted movement from your running stride. Strength training, in particular, makes the hip, knee, and ankle joints less wobbly and thus decreases the amount of energy that is dissipated with each footstrike.

Also, strength training, as well as other activities such as cycling that have a strengthening effect beyond that of running, improves running performance by increasing a runner's power. More power means a stronger push-off, longer strides, and the ability to run faster at any given cadence. Greater strength in the core muscles (the lower back and abdomen) enhances running power, too, by enhancing the transfer of forces between the upper body and the legs, a component of running whose importance is often overlooked (just try running without moving your arms!).

Finally, there's the volume factor. Running has always been a low-volume sport in comparison to other endurance sports like swimming and cycling. Elite swimmers often swim 4 or more hours a day, while elite cyclists train upwards of 6 hours a day during certain periods. By contrast, elite marathoners, even the so-called mega-mileage ones, seldom train more than 90 minutes a day—if all they do is run. The reason is, of course, that running causes much more wear and tear on the body than swimming and cycling. But by cross-training in nonimpact endurance disciplines, runners can substantially increase the overall cardiovascular conditioning stimulus they receive with little extra wear and tear.

Now, you don't have to be running 90 minutes a day already to enjoy this benefit. Anyone who is doing, or who sometimes does, about as much running as he or she can handle, regardless of the quantity, can take advantage of it. In fact, the *less* running you do, the more your fitness will improve when you add endurance cross-training workouts.

You can even *decrease* your weekly mileage slightly while increasing your overall exercise volume through cross-training and wind up in better shape. In any case, the key to success is easing into this higher volume very gradually. Add just one or two gentle workouts at first, do it for a few weeks, see how it goes, and then perhaps add another.

Better efficiency, more strength and power, and greater training volume without additional breakdown—these are the ways in which cross-training directly boosts running fitness. But I should mention that all of the other reasons to cross-train discussed in this chapter have a beneficial, if indirect, impact on performance. I mentioned, for example, that cross-training can reduce injuries. This allows you to train more consistently, and that, of course, makes you better prepared to race. Using cross-training for active recovery (reason number 4, discussed below) can enhance your recovery between key workouts, so you perform better in your key workouts, get a more powerful training effect from them, and again achieve a higher level of fitness by race day. And so forth.

BENEFIT #4: ACTIVE RECOVERY

Working out does not increase one's fitness level. *Recovering* from workouts does. By itself, an individual workout is nothing more than a stressor that harms the body. What would happen if you tried to work

DEENA KASTOR

Deena Kastor (formerly Deena Drossin) is widely considered the best female American distance runner to come along since Joan Benoit. By the year 2000, Kastor was certainly the best female American distance runner actively competing. That year, she won the U.S. Olympic Trials 10,000 meters and the U.S. Cross-Country Championships at both the 4-K and 8-K distances. The following year, she set an American debut marathon record of 2:26:58.

But Kastor was not satisfied, because she seldom faired as well against the best in the world as she did against the best at home. Her top rivals from Europe, Asia, and Africa were just a few steps ahead of her, and she wanted to close the gap. Wise enough to know she could not achieve a different result by doing the same thing, Kastor tried something new, incorporating plyometrics and core strength training into her preparations for her 2002 racing.

The results speak for themselves. Kastor began the year by claiming a silver medal in the World Cross-Country Championships 8-K. She followed that by setting a world 5-K road record (14:54) and an American record for 10,000 meters (30:50:32). Whenever she was asked how she had achieved such a breakthrough year, Kastor credited the extra power and efficiency she had developed through strength training and plyometrics above all other factors. In 2003, Kastor's roll continued as she set new American records in the 15-K and marathon.

out nonstop, every minute of every day? You'd wake up in the hospital, if you were lucky.

It is an irrefutable but too often overlooked fact that workouts help you achieve athletic conditioning only when followed by rest and recovery-promoting activities. (Obviously, nutrition and hydration play major roles in recovery, but I want to keep our discussion focused on exercise.)

So we know there's a difference between conditioning and simply beating up your body. Training is useful only when you allow your body to "absorb" it before you train again. Each individual workout pulls your body away from homeostasis (or equilibrium) in various ways: by depleting your muscles' fuel stores, damaging muscles and connective tissues, and so forth. Your body absorbs a workout when it returns to homeostasis during the period of rest that follows the workout. It replenishes fuel stores, rebuilds damaged tissues, et cetera. Fitness increases when your body's systems are able to go *beyond* their original abilities, when they become better able to handle the kinds of stress you put on them in workouts. This process happens during the recovery period, not during the workout.

Take the example of fuel storage. The primary source of energy for running is carbohydrate stored in the form of glycogen in skeletal muscle and the liver. Working out depletes these fuel stores, usually partially, sometimes completely. After workouts, your body gradually replenishes its glycogen supply using carbohydrate from the food you eat. Over time, as your body is repeatedly challenged in this way, it learns to store greater amounts of glycogen in the muscles and liver, thereby making it harder to deplete them in future workouts and races and increasing your endurance. This is just one of many ways in which the human body absorbs training stimuli. This adaptation is called supercompensation. And the most important thing to remember about supercompensation is that it happens during your downtime between workouts.

However, outright rest is not the only vehicle of recovery and adaptation. In fact, even in the example I just gave, it's not inactivity alone but rather the combination of inactivity and the activity of consuming carbohydrate that facilitates the adaptation of increased glycogen storage. Like proper sports nutrition, low-intensity workouts can also facilitate recovery and adaptation. They do so in part by increasing bloodflow, and with it the delivery of nutrients to the muscles and the clearing of metabolic wastes from them, and in part by stimulating the recovery process more frequently, as most of the physical adaptations that constitute increased fitness occur in the first hours after a workout.

Periods of outright rest are, of course, essential, but the runner who performs active-recovery workouts between most pairs of key workouts will become fitter than the runner who does not, provided he or she has gradually worked toward being able to handle the frequency of training involved. While the runner who does not perform active-recovery workouts gets more rest than the runner who does, it's actually the latter who gets more recovery. Again, this is primarily because the 2 hours immediately following a workout are far more valuable to most adaptive processes (including our example of glycogen storage) than are the hours following those first 2. It may be counterintuitive, but it's true nevertheless that in the context of a rigorous training program, light workouts accelerate recovery beyond what happens during outright rest by just slightly increasing the body's need for recovery.

Low-intensity running is a suitable form of active recovery from key run workouts, but nonimpact forms of cardiovascular exercise may be even better. First, and most obviously, they challenge the aerobic system without further beating up your body's joints and connective tissues, which can handle only so much pavement pounding. Second, you can present your aerobic-energy system with a greater challenge than you could get in a low-intensity jog. In other words, if you're bicycling or inline skating, you can dial it up a bit and still promote recovery from running while increasing your overall fitness level.

Put another way, a low-intensity cross-training workout, of short or moderate duration, can promote recovery without in any way retarding it. However, a short, easy run could promote recovery in some ways (increasing bloodflow and the need for enhanced glycogen storage) but also prevent recovery, because it puts more wear and tear on tissues that are already beaten up from more strenuous runs.

I won't go so far as to suggest that all of your easy workouts should be performed in disciplines other than running. Ultimately, nothing makes you a better runner than running does. Every competitive runner should run at least three times a week. So if you do four cardiovascular workouts a week, only one of them should be a cross-training workout, even if two or three of your weekly workouts are easy. Similarly, highly competitive runners training for optimal performance should run at least six times a week. Yet even a highly competitive runner cannot handle more than four hard runs per week, so at least two of that athlete's weekly runs should be easy, regardless of how many additional cross-training workouts he or she does.

Your key workouts—that is, your high-intensity workouts and your extra-long workouts—are the most important to your running performance, so those should almost always be runs. When you're injured, you should perform cross-training workouts that match your intended run workouts in duration, structure, and intensity. But if you can run, you

DAVID KRUMMENACKER

David Krummenacker is the best American male combined 800-meter/1500-meter runner of all time. But before active-recovery cross-training workouts became an important component of his training regimen at age 26, he was merely a very good middle-distance runner.

When he finished 12th in the 2000 Olympic Trials 1500 meters, Krummenacker held personal bests of 3:35:15 in that event and 1:44:57 in the 800. The following year, desperate for a key to unlock the door to the next level, he hired a new coach. Luiz de Oliviera, a Brazilian who had coached half-miler Joachim Cruz to a gold medal at the 1984 Olympics, surprised Krummenacker by reducing his training volume and adding weekly active-recovery pool runs into his training.

As a result, Krummenacker found himself feeling fresher for his hard track workouts and thus performing better. He began the 2002 season by establishing a new American indoor record at 1000 meters (2:17). Before the year was out, he had won a national championship at 800 meters; lowered his personal bests to 1:43:95 in the 800, 2:15:97 in the 1000, and 3:31:93 in the 1500; and won two major 800-meter races on the European circuit against the world's best. The following year he stepped it up another notch, becoming the indoor world champion at 800 meters.

While he maintained that a variety of factors contributed to his great breakthrough, Krummenacker felt that the pool running was as important a factor as any. Nor was this the only form of cross-training he took up in preparation for his breakout season. Plyometrics was another, which, he said, made him stronger in the final 200 meters at all distances.

will be best served to make all of your key workouts runs and all of your endurance cross-training workouts active-recovery sessions.

BENEFIT #5: ENHANCED MOTIVATION

No matter how much passion you have for running, if you do it often enough or with excessive repetition of routes and routines, it will become boring. Most humans are stimulated by variety and turned off by monotony. Cross-training helps you maintain your enthusiasm for your sport, making it possible to train harder and more consistently and ultimately to perform better in races.

Anything you can do to increase your motivation for training is worth doing. In other words, a given training decision does not have to be justified by a purely physical rationale to be a good decision. If doing more cross-training and less running makes the training process more enjoyable, do it! Likewise, if you just don't feel like running today, but you would be perfectly happy to ski cross-country instead, then ski! You'll still end up in a better place than the runner who doesn't cross-train and can choose only, on such days, between running with a bad attitude and doing nothing at all.

BENEFIT #6: REJUVENATION

No tree can bear fruit in all seasons, and no runner can train hard throughout the entire calendar. That's just the way nature made us. If you want to run better next year than you did this year, you must give your body and mind a break from formal training after the final race. Coaches call this period of rest and play the transition phase of the training cycle, and every smart runner takes it as seriously (if one can take rest and play seriously) as he or she does any other phase of training.

A good off-season transition phase (which usually coincides with winter) should begin with about 2 weeks of complete rest. Fourteen exertion-free days are just enough to allow your body to achieve a deep recovery from the recently completed training cycle and to restore your hunger to run, but not so much that you seriously compromise your fitness.

After resting for 2 weeks, you should allow yourself between 2 and 8

STEVE PLASENCIA

Few runners have been able to run so well for so long as Steve Plasencia. In a professional career that lasted from the early 1980s to the mid-1990s, Plasencia made two Olympic teams and narrowly missed making a third (he placed fourth in the 1996 Olympic Trials Marathon). He finished as high as 10th in the World Championships 10,000 meters and established a personal best of 27:45 in that event. After turning 40, Plasencia broke five masters records.

But Plasencia's career had its low points. He dropped out of the 1988 Olympic 10,000 meters with a stress fracture that left him unable to walk without crutches for several weeks. A former youth hockey player, Plasencia decided to keep fit by inline skating. He enjoyed it so much, and it served him so well, that he decided to keep it in his training regimen even after his injury had healed.

Every Monday, after his Sunday long run, Plasencia skated a 25-mile loop near his home in Eugene, Oregon, at a moderately high intensity level. Because it involved no impact, the workout helped his tissues recover from his long run. But its duration and intensity provided a greater challenge to his cardiorespiratory and metabolic systems than he would have been able to manage with running alone.

In addition, Plasencia found that his weekly skate was often one of his most eagerly anticipated workouts. It gave his body and his mind a break from pounding the pavement and circling the track. As a result, Plasencia returned to competition from his injury feeling invigorated physically and psychologically. The following year, at 33, he set a new career-best time of 13:19 for 5000 meters.

Libbie Hickman was one of the best American distance runners of the 1990s. She posted personal-best times of 15:11 for 5000 meters, 31:41 for 10,000 meters, and 2:28:34 in the marathon. She won many major road races, such as the Boulder Bolder, and she made the Olympic final at 10,000 meters in the 2000 Games.

While attending Colorado State University, Hickman (then Libbie Johnson) was introduced to cross-country skiing, for which she quickly developed a passion that nearly rivaled her passion for running. Throughout her professional running career, Hickman returned to skis during the winter, at first just because she couldn't resist, but later for the additional reason that she came to view this cross-training period as one of the most important and beneficial parts of her year-round training program.

Hickman would ski every day—often all day—2 to 3 weeks per month for approximately 2 months each winter. All this skiing allowed her to maintain or even increase her basic cardiovascular fitness while giving her mind and body a badly needed break from running. By the time she returned to regular run training in late winter, she felt physically stronger and emotionally recharged, ready on all levels for the long stretch of hard training and high-stakes racing that lay ahead.

more weeks of informal training in which you do whatever you want. Play basketball or ice hockey, do yoga, swim, lift weights—and run as little or as much (within reason) as you see fit. Your first priority should simply be to enjoy yourself. As long as you do some form of workout each day and get a cardiovascular, strength, and flexibility benefit from the activity or group of activities you pursue, there's no wrong way to approach the transition phase.

BENEFIT #7: ENJOYING OTHER SPORTS

Endurance is a highly transferable capacity. The strong heart and good lungs that serve you so well as a runner could serve you equally well in swimming, bicycling, skating, cross-country skiing, and other endurance sports. Yet endurance is also highly task-specific, because the only way to develop efficiency in a given activity is to perform that activity often. So while a trained runner would undoubtedly perform better on a bicycle than a couch potato would, that runner wouldn't fare so well against a trained cyclist.

Genetic individuality is also a factor. Because various muscular, neurological, and metabolic characteristics of your body are the way they are, you may never be as good a cyclist as you are a runner no matter how much cycling you do. On the other hand, you could merely dabble in cycling and discover that you are even better suited to that sport than you are to running.

You never know until you try. And I'm here to suggest that you do try if you have the least bit of curiosity about what it might be like to compete in another endurance sport. You might really enjoy the experience and do well, and if you do it right, training for and competing in a second endurance sport could help you enjoy running more and even run better.

A sensible way to begin is by performing recovery workouts in some discipline in which you might someday like to race. Your body will quickly begin to adapt to the new sport, you will develop good technique, and you will gather a sense of just how much you do in fact enjoy it and whether you have an aptitude for it.

The next step would be to participate in a short, low-key race in the new sport. In order to be adequately prepared for it, you would need to perform at least three workouts per week in it, and some of these workouts would need to be longer and harder than your typical recovery workout. You can take it as far as you want.

As I mentioned in the introduction to this book, I myself do a fairly even mixture of triathlons and running events, but I'm always focused on one or the other. When I'm training for a marathon, I do a few swim and bike recovery workouts each week. When I'm preparing for a big triathlon, I reduce my running workload, increase my swimming and cycling workloads, and train equally hard in all three disciplines. This system works well for me, as I enjoy the competition as well as the activities themselves.

Because triathlon seems to be the crossover sport of choice for runners (probably because it actually involves running), I've included a triathlon-training program for runners among the various programs presented in chapter 7.

BENEFIT #8: FIT PREGNANCY

In the not-too-distant past, exercising throughout pregnancy and soon after childbirth was considered dangerous, and motherhood was considered to be a career-ending decision for competitive female athletes. These notions were, of course, based on presumption rather than observation, and they have since gone the way of the notion that women lacked the strength and stamina to run a marathon.

If you are a woman who's physically fit at the time of conception, you can safely exercise throughout your entire pregnancy, and your labor will likely be easier and your child healthier for it. You can ease back into an exercise routine within a week to 10 days of giving birth, if all goes well.

Cross-training can help pregnant and postpartum runners in a couple of ways. Running becomes difficult for some women during the last several weeks of pregnancy, and high-intensity running becomes impossible for most women during this period. Staying aerobically fit is as simple as substituting nonimpact endurance activities for running. You may wish to make this transition even in the absence of discomfort during running, just in case. There's really no downside to doing so.

Approach the final week or two before your due date much as you would a marathon, as (it's often been remarked) giving birth is much like running a marathon. In other words, rest up. After childbirth, your body will be ready for stretching and nonimpact forms of cardiovascular exercise before you're ready to run, so if you're itching to do something, cross-train first and then start running when your body tells you you're ready for it.

Strength training, especially for your core muscles, can not only make carrying and delivering a child easier but can also facilitate your return to running after delivery by keeping your joints strong and your bones dense. If you haven't strength-trained consistently in the past, use pregnancy as your motivation to start, and then stick with it.

Most active women find that they can do more and stay fitter during

NED OVEREND

Ned Overend got his start as a runner, but if he had stayed a runner, he never would have known the feeling of being the best in the world at something—let alone more than one thing. And he never would have enjoyed the fame and fortune that accrue to the best.

A Colorado native, Overend ran a 4:12 mile in high school and later got into mountain running. He finished second in the 1980 Pikes Peak Marathon and repeated the performance the following year. Also in 1980, fatefully, a friend talked Overend into competing in the third annual Hawaii Ironman Triathlon (2.4-mile swim/112-mile bike ride/26.2-mile run).

Overend came away from the experience with a newfound taste for cycling, and by 1983 he was racing bikes professionally, whereas making a living as a runner had never been a possibility for him. The following year, Overend made a foray into the fledgling sport of mountain biking, emerging as the National Championships runner-up. Thus began a storied off-road career that brought him six National Championships titles and a gold medal in the inaugural UCI (Union Cycliste Internationale) World Championship in 1991 at age 36.

In 1996, after representing the United States in the first-ever Olympic Cross-Country Mountain Bike Race, Overend officially retired from mountain bike racing. But he kept riding, and he got back into running, and he even started working on his swim technique for the first time in a while. Before long, he was dabbling in another new endurance sport: off-road triathlon.

That same year, his 41st on earth, Overend finished third in the Xterra Triathlon Championships, the unofficial world championship of off-road triathlon. The next year, he took second, and then, incredibly, he won the event twice in a row, at 43 and 44, against rivals a decade and more younger than he. Since then, it's been no overstatement to call Overend one of the greatest multisport endurance athletes of all time.

If anyone ever told the great Irish runner Sonia O'Sullivan that pregnancy and athletics don't mix, she didn't listen. Twice during her long reign as perhaps the world's best all-around distance runner (she excelled on the track, on the roads, and in cross-country), O'Sullivan took time off to have a child. Twice she bore healthy babies and returned to world-class form within a few short months after labor.

O'Sullivan gave birth to her first child in July 1999. By October of that year, she was racing again, and the following summer she won an Olympic silver medal at 5000 meters—something she'd failed to do in two previous Olympic appearances. In December 2001, O'Sullivan had a second child, and just 13 weeks later, she finished seventh in the Cross-Country World Championship.

Cross-training helped O'Sullivan stay fit throughout both of her pregnancies. As her belly grew, she gradually reduced the volume and intensity of her running, but the less running she did, the more indoor cycling she did to compensate. She also lifted weights more often than usual and felt that the additional strength she gained prepared her body to handle a quick ramp-up in her run training after giving birth. The results speak for themselves.

---

pregnancy than they thought (and had been told) they could, and can bounce back faster as well. Still, there are those highly committed runners who would like pregnancy to be less of an interruption than it really must be. All of the runner-mothers I've talked with agree that regardless of what's physically possible, it's best for running to take a backseat to baby for the year surrounding childbirth. Don't expect or try to race at a high level during this time. Listen to your body and remember your priorities.

I hope I've made a convincing case for making the transition to a cross-training—based program. It's a tough sell to many runners, because it's running that we love to do most. But your love of running can be the very thing that motivates you to begin cross-training once you realize how much this approach can benefit your running health, fitness, and performance.

In the next three chapters, I will show you how to get started in each of the three cross-training modalities: strength training, flexibility training, and endurance cross-training. Let's begin with strength training since it is the most unfamiliar form of cross-training for many runners.

STRENGTH TRAINING

WE RUNNERS ARE NOTORIOUSLY reluctant to strength-train. A typical runner has about as much interest in hitting the gym as the average powerlifter has in hitting the track. The three reasons runners commonly give for resisting resistance exercise are fears of "bulking up," a perceived lack of time and energy to devote to it, and the belief that strength training offers no particular benefits to runners.

Wrong, wrong, and wrong again! The truth is that an appropriate strength program will add no weight to your body, require a minimal time commitment, and make you a better, healthier runner.

Let me take a moment to dismantle these three common objections more thoroughly. First of all, it's nearly impossible to gain any significant amount of muscle mass as long as you're engaged in daily or near-daily aerobic exercise, even if you're trying to bulk up. Resistance training tends to increase the size of individual muscle fibers (which, in the aggregate, is what causes bulking up), whereas endurance training has the opposite effect. When the two forms of training are combined, they more or less cancel each other out on this level. I know this from experience. As a senior in high school who ran about 40 miles a week and lifted weights on the side, I stood 6 feet 1 inch and weighed all of 138 pounds. After the fall cross-country season, I burned out and quit running but continued lifting weights. I gained 34 pounds in 10 weeks—and I've got the stretch marks to prove it! Formal studies conducted by exercise scientists have demonstrated that these cause-and-effect relationships are not unique to me.

Nor is time an issue. Runners can achieve substantive benefits from a very small amount of strength training—as little as 40 minutes a week, if it's a consistent 40 minutes. Also, runners can perform a greater amount of strength training during the winter off-season, when more time is available, and maintain the associated benefits throughout the competitive season by performing a lesser, "maintenance" level of strength training.

The primary benefits of strength training for runners are injury prevention and improved running performance. What more could you ask for? There are many examples of runners who have overcome chronic fragility and effected major performance breakthroughs by incorporating resistance exercise. I keep a file on them. One such case is that of the great cross-country runner Pat Porter. A good but not exceptional athlete in high school, Porter became, in the early 1980s, one of the first elite runners to begin giving more than lip service to strength training. His strength carried him to an incredible eight consecutive national championship titles in cross-country between 1982 and 1989.

But if such stories are so common (and yes, I really do keep a file on them), then why doesn't strength training enjoy a widespread reputation for benefiting runners? One reason is that few runners give resistance training an honest chance. You need to do it consistently and correctly for many weeks before the benefits will manifest themselves, and most runners aren't so patient with an activity they approach with skepticism and little enthusiasm.

A second and related reason is that few runners strength-train correctly, because few are taught the appropriate approach to lifting. Runners should do two kinds of resistance exercise: corrective and functional. Corrective exercises are those that strengthen important stabilizing muscles that are typically left underdeveloped in runners and in which weakness often leads to overuse injuries. Functional exercises are those that simulate aspects or components of the running stride, under load. Performing them leads to a more powerful running stride and better running performance.

Until very recently, nobody bothered to figure out which resistance exercises were most corrective or functional for runners. The majority of strength-training experts had no interest in or knowledge about running, and the majority of running experts knew and cared nothing about strength training. Even today, only a minority of trainers and coaches knows how to prescribe a truly corrective and functional strength program for running.

My goal in this chapter is to provide you with just such a program. I'll show you a number of corrective and functional strength exercises for runners and also how to construct three distinct types of workouts using this pool of exercises. Finally, I'll show how to string together these workouts to create a year-round strength program that will complement your running.

First, though, I'd like to say a few more words about how strength training can help you avoid injuries and improve your running performance. This knowledge will, I think, both motivate you to strength-train and assist you in making informed decisions about how you do it.

THE IMPORTANCE OF MUSCLE BALANCE

Muscle weakness is a factor in a majority of the overuse injuries that runners experience. Here's how it happens. (Brace yourself for a little physiology.) In a cyclical movement pattern such as running, certain muscles act mainly to generate movement while other muscles act mainly to provide stability.

The main force-producing muscles in running are:

- **The gastrocnemius and the soleus (the two large muscles of the calf, also called the plantar flexors)**

- **The hamstrings (the muscles on the back of the thigh) and the hip flexors (the muscles that join the thigh to the pelvis and spine on the front of the leg and torso)**

The main stabilizing muscles are:

- **The quadriceps (a group of four muscles on the front of the thigh, which help mainly to keep the knees stable)**

- **The tibialis anterior and other dorsiflexors (on the front and inside of the shin)**

- **The hip abductors (on the outer side of the hip, which keep the pelvis in place)**

(continued on page 30)

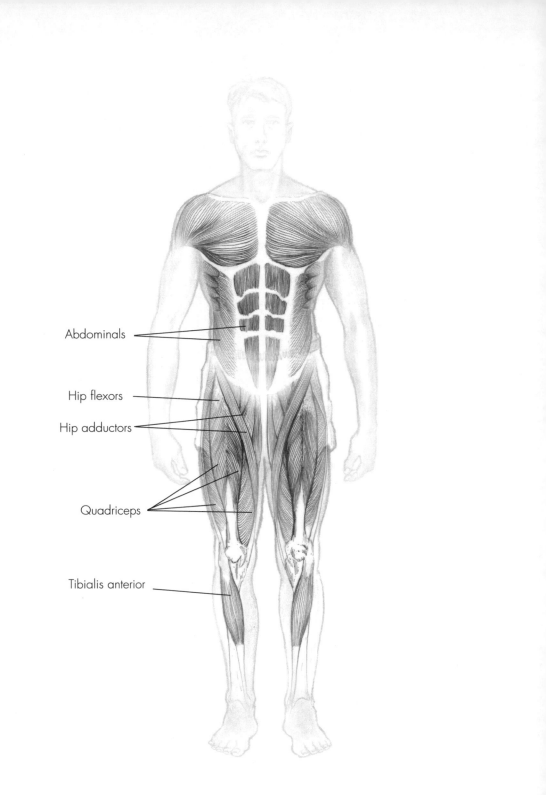

Abdominals

Hip flexors

Hip adductors

Quadriceps

Tibialis anterior

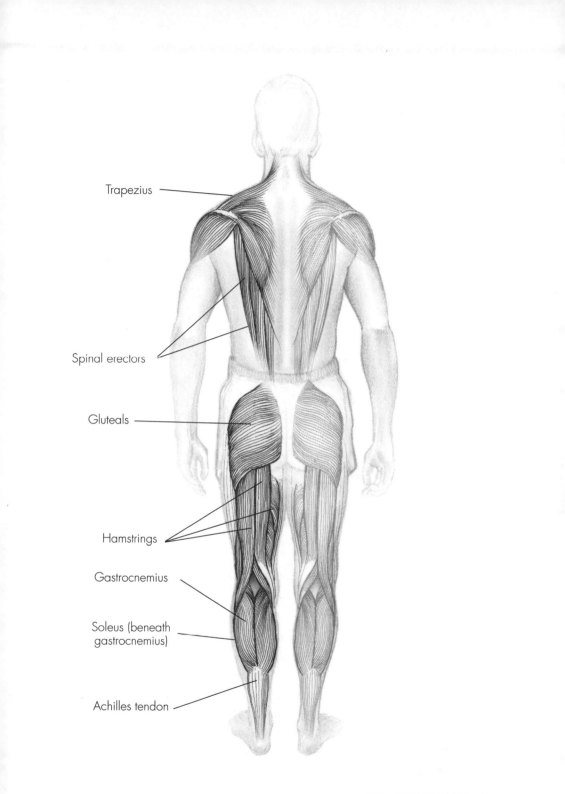

Trapezius

Spinal erectors

Gluteals

Hamstrings

Gastrocnemius

Soleus (beneath
gastrocnemius)

Achilles tendon

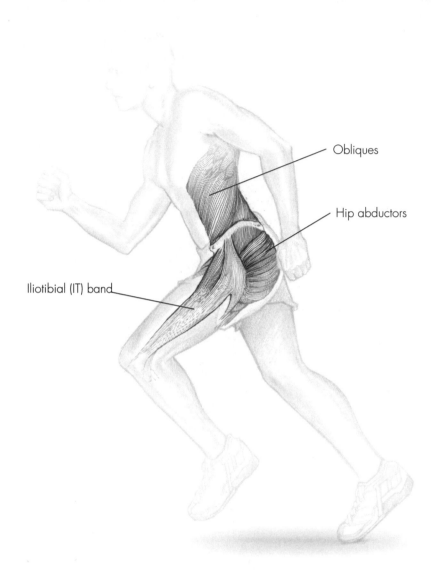

Obliques

Hip abductors

Iliotibial (IT) band

- **The abdominals, spinal erectors, and other muscles of the lower trunk (which help you maintain an upright posture)**

In running, the muscles in charge of generating movement do a lot more work than those whose main job is to provide stability. Consequently, over time, the movers tend to become a lot stronger, while the stabilizers don't. Eventually, the movers can become so overdeveloped in relation to the stabilizers that they actually start to take over the

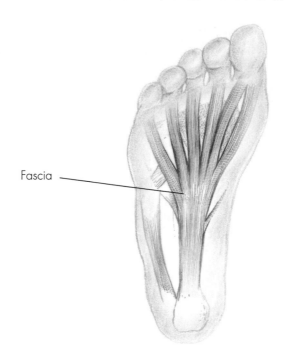

Fascia

duty of joint stabilization, even though they aren't designed to do this during running. Such imbalances can lead to biomechanical abnormalities, joint instability, and eventual dysfunction.

Three of the most common running injuries—Achilles tendinitis, plantar fasciitis, and shin splints—are frequently associated with an imbalance in the muscles of the lower leg. Once again, in running, the muscles on the back of the lower leg (the gastrocnemius and the soleus, also called plantar flexors) are movers, while the tibialis anterior and other dorsiflexors on the front and inside of the shin act primarily as stabilizers. Repetitive running leads to overdevelopment of the calf muscles in relation to the dorsiflexors, such that the latter are no longer able to properly stabilize the ankle.

This instability, in turn, can allow the foot to overpronate—that is, to roll inward excessively during the footstrike. Overpronation puts a lot of strain on the **Achilles tendon**, which typically becomes tightened along with the calf muscles in runners. The frequent result is the pain and inflammation that signal Achilles tendinitis.

Overpronation can also overstretch the web of protective connective tissue (called **fascia**) on the bottom of the foot, causing the heel-pain condition known as plantar fasciitis. The small muscles on the inside part of the shin can also tear as a consequence of overpronation, an injury familiar to many runners as a shin splint.

Other common muscle-imbalance problems start with the bigger muscles. The hamstrings are prime movers in the running stride. Consequently, they tend to become strong and tight in runners while the quadriceps, which are needed for proper stabilization, remain relatively undeveloped. Two types of overuse injury commonly result. Hamstring strains are small tears, usually in the upper part of a hamstring muscle. (Note that three separate muscles comprise the hamstrings, which are treated as a single muscle unit because these three muscles always act together.) Patellafemoral pain syndrome ("runner's knee") is a bruising of the kneecap that results from improper tracking of the kneecap during the running stride.

Another type of imbalance injury starts at the hip joint and affects a strip of connective tissue every runner has heard of: the **iliotibial, or IT, band.** Here's how it happens:

The hip abductors—the muscles on the sides of your gluteals and upper thighs—are important running stabilizers. The hip abductors on your left leg prevent the right side of your pelvis from tilting toward the ground when your left foot is planted and your right foot is off the ground, and then the abductors on your right leg return the favor when your left foot is off the ground. Neither running nor anything the average runner does in everyday life develops these muscles. Their weakness affects the IT band, which is the body's largest tendon and runs from the hip joint down past the knee joint on the outside of the leg. The lateral pelvic tilt associated with weak abductors causes this tendon to rub against the femur (thighbone) and become inflamed, a condition known as iliotibial band syndrome.

Yet another common muscle imbalance in runners is anterior (forward) pelvic tilt. This condition, associated with weak lower abdominal muscles and overstretched lower back muscles, is generally caused by habitual sitting, which is why a majority of adults in our society, runners and nonrunners alike, exhibit this imbalance. Anterior pelvic tilt contributes to overpronation, which, as you already know, contributes to several types of overuse injury. This imbalance also tends to shorten your running stride and increase the duration of each footstrike, thereby slowing you down. And slow is bad.

ALAN WEBB

Alan Webb became an American running hero at the tender age of 18 when, in 2001, he broke Jim Ryun's long-standing high school mile record by running 3:53:43 at the Prefontaine Classic in Oregon.

One of Webb's greatest assets as a runner is his strength. You can see this not only in the way he drives through the bell lap of a mile race but even when he's standing at the starting line. He's one of the most muscular elite runners you'll ever see.

Webb, under the guidance of his coach, Scott Raczko, also puts more effort into strength training than most other runners. In some periods of his training, he spends as much time working on strength, power, and flexibility as he does actually running. He practices a variety of strength-training modalities, including weight lifting, body-weight exercises (pushups, bar dips, et cetera), core-muscle work using a medicine ball, plyometrics, stride drills, hill running, and the use of a wobble board to strengthen his shins. Even more unusual, Webb often does long, multimodality workouts in which a run is immediately preceded and followed by extensive strength and flexibility work.

After his Cinderella year as a high school senior, Webb suffered through a couple of tough years in which he raced poorly, dropped out of his first college, suffered injuries, and even had an emergency appendectomy. Many observers began to write him off as a one-hit wonder. I believe Webb has many great feats ahead of him (he's still in his early twenties), not least of all because of his commitment to smart cross-training.

Strength training prevents injuries in a pretty straightforward manner. By subjecting your running antagonists and stabilizers to resistance outside the context of running, you make these muscles stronger and better able to do the job they're designed to do during running. This takes strain off the prime movers and synergists, supports proper biomechanics, and enhances the stability of the joints.

GYM TOYS

Resistance bands. These can be as simple as lengths of surgical tubing. The best type of band for resistance exercise has a handle at either end, plus an attachment in the middle that allows you to insert it into a door frame. Bands come in various ranges of thickness and/or tension for different degrees of resistance. I recommend getting two bands for the sake of versatility.

Tell your fitness-equipment retailer how you plan to use your bands and, frankly, about how strong you are, and he or she should be able to match you up with the right ones. The best online functional-fitness-gear sites (such as www.performbetter.com) should offer some guidelines before you give up the plastic. Two sets of bands could cost from $20 to $50. (You get what you pay for.)

Bands offer a different form of resistance than traditional weights. Where a barbell or dumbbell will often be easiest to move near the end of the exercise, when the battle against gravity has been won, a band will be most difficult to pull near the end, when tension is highest. Bands score high on portability (they fit in a suitcase without adding much more weight than an extra pair of running shoes), storability (they'll hang in a closet just fine), and cost.

Important note: If you work out in a gym or have a multistation home-gym apparatus, you can use a cable pulley and weight-stack system (or a Bowflex-type machine, if you have one) to do resistance-band exercises. Make sure the pulley machine you use has high, medium, and low positions. You want to be able to start with the cable at your feet, shoulders, or head.

Medicine ball. A medicine ball provides a versatile form of resistance that adds challenge to movements that otherwise might not be challenging enough. Standard medicine balls are volleyball- to basketball-size and

come in weights ranging from 6 to 20 pounds. A 12-pound ball offers the greatest versatility but may be too heavy for certain twisting movements and too light for other movements. You may want to purchase a lighter ball and a heavier one. The heavier balls are only marginally larger than the smaller ones. Expect to pay $60 to $90 for a long-lasting ball. Some fitness clubs have these as well.

Dumbbells. Dumbbells are the iron in "pumping iron." They are, as you're probably aware, pure-metal, handheld forms of resistance that are sold in pairs by weight. The smallest ones are 2 pounds and the largest are . . . well, let's just say they're heavier than anything you'll ever lift.

The chief advantage of dumbbells is that they are compact and take up little space. Their main drawback is that you need several pairs in order to be able to perform a variety of exercises with appropriate resistance, and they're not as cheap as you might think.

For example, a complete set of dumbbells from 5 to 50 pounds, with a rack, will probably cost you close to $250. Adjustable dumbbells (you buy the handles and weights separately) are cheaper but require a lot of fuss to change the weight between exercises. The "selectorized" dumbbells, such as PowerBlock and IronMaster Quick/Change, are much easier to use and store but run several hundred dollars for the basic set and a stand to rest them on.

Your problem is solved if you work out at a health club, which will have every size of dumbbell you could ever hope to use.

Exercise bench. A few of the exercises described in this chapter require the use of a 12- to 18-inch-high support platform. A basic, flat exercise bench is perfectly suited for the job. (You can get one for as

little as $100 at discount retailers or online.) Another option is to stack a few plastic "steps" such as those used for step aerobics. If you'd rather save a few bucks, a sturdy chair will suffice.

THE STRENGTH-SPEED CONNECTION

If muscle imbalances led only to overuse injuries, they'd be bad enough. But they also reduce a runner's energy efficiency with every stride. Overpronation, for example, is a big waste of energy. The foot goes sideways when you're trying to run forward. This prolongs ground contact and decreases the amount of force you're able to generate for push-off. Similarly, the instability in the knee joint that comes along with imbalance in the thigh musculature causes energy to be lost every time the foot lands, because the knee wobbles ever so slightly. By strengthening the underdeveloped running stabilizers, you can improve your energy efficiency and run faster. And faster is good.

Muscle strength is inherently beneficial to runners, even if you separate it from its connection with muscle balance. Running ability is generally considered to be a function of how much oxygen one can consume per unit of time ("aerobic capacity") and how little energy one can burn while running at any given pace ("economy"). However, given two runners who have the same aerobic capacity and matching economy, the faster of the two will be the runner with stronger running muscles.

Running speed is a function of stride length and rate. Strong runners can take longer strides more rapidly. Hence, as a runner, you want to be as strong (in the running muscles) as you can be without sacrificing aerobic capacity and economy. Now, if you were to do 90 percent strength training and 10 percent running, you would get a lot stronger, but you would also lose aerobic capacity (due to insufficient aerobic stimulus) and economy (due to weight gain and another factor having to do with muscle fiber types that's too complex to explain between parentheses, so take my word for it). You'd wind up a slower runner. But if you reverse this ratio, you'll gain a modest amount of strength, maintain your aerobic capacity and economy, and become a faster runner.

And if you're over 30, the age at which men and women tend to start losing muscle mass and strength if they don't take action, you should strength-train for reasons completely aside from your interest in running. You can actually reverse the age-related loss of muscle and strength for a while, turning back the physiological clock, and afterward slow it considerably.

TRAINING TO MOVE

For most of us, strength training is synonymous with bodybuilding. We think of exercises to build individual muscles, like biceps curls and triceps extensions. But let's get one thing clear from the outset: As a runner, you should not strength-train like a bodybuilder. Performing exercises that isolate and concentrate force upon muscles separately results in big muscles that look powerful but are virtually incapable of cooperating with each other to perform athletic movements.

Runners (and, indeed, all athletes) should train movements, not individual muscles. A majority of the exercises you perform should simulate and intensify some action that your body performs in running, because your goal is to make your running movers better able to generate force during running and to make your running stabilizers better able to stabilize during running. In other words, these exercises must be functional.

A classic bodybuilding exercise like the barbell bench press, with its full-trunk stabilization, muscular isolation, and symmetrical limb movements, simulates nothing you'll ever do on a road, track, or trail. (As a two-joint movement—elbows and shoulders—the barbell bench doesn't isolate muscles to the degree that many other bodybuilding exercises do, but it's still only marginally functional.) Functional strength training is all about training your body to perform sport-specific movements with correct form and greater force. Like running itself, your key strength-training exercises should involve balance, independent limb movements, and cooperation among several muscles that are centrally involved in the running stride.

There are five component movements of the running stride: heel raising, lunging, bending, twisting, and pushing and pulling. Heel raising—plantar flexion—occurs when the toes "plant" and force the heel off the ground. The lunging movement entails a forward thrust with one leg and a lifting, reaching, and planting of the other. Runners do not (and should not) "bend" at the waist per se, but they do maintain an upright posture that requires work from the bending muscles: the abdominals and the spinal erectors. The same muscles, plus the obliques, engage in twisting a runner's torso slightly from side to side, which is essential for the transfer of forces between the upper and lower body. Lastly, the arms push and pull in opposition to the legs for balance and supplemental force generation.

In addition to functional exercises, a second type of resistance exercise you should include in your strength program is the corrective type, whose purpose is to strengthen weak stabilizers. Corrective exercises are sometimes more like bodybuilding exercises in that they do isolate individual muscles or muscle groups. However, they are performed not for the sake of maximizing muscle growth but rather for the sake of enhancing the ability of certain muscles to function as stabilizers in running. It's possible for exercises to be functional and corrective at the same time, and in fact all of the strength exercises I'll present here are both functional and corrective in relation to running except for those labeled as "Corrective Exercises for the Lower-Leg Stabilizers," which are strictly corrective.

After I've shown you the exercises, I'll explain how to use them to create three types of strength workouts—specifically, light, heavy, and power workouts—and, from these, a year-round strength program that will reduce overuse injuries and improve your running ability. Note that beneath the name of each exercise (again, with the exception of corrective exercises for the lower-leg stabilizers), information is given about the workout type or types (light, heavy, and/or power) for which this particular exercise is suited. Naturally, you'll be able to make better sense of this information once I've described these three workout types. I'll get into recommended loads, repetitions, and sets when I discuss these three workout types as well.

Some of the exercises presented here require the use of a resistance band, a few call for dumbbells, others require a medicine ball, and still others require a stable support such as an exercise bench or step.

PLANTAR FLEXION EXERCISES

If the running stride begins anywhere, it begins at the ankle. You need strong, efficient calf muscles that can flex the ankle powerfully and repetitively to produce the long, rapid strides that are the essence of fast running. These plantar flexion exercises will help you develop those muscles.

STANDING CALF RAISE
(LIGHT, HEAVY)

Benefits: The standing calf raise strengthens the calf muscles, yielding a more powerful push-off in the running stride.

Procedure: Stand facing a 12- to 18-inch-high support platform (such as an exercise bench) with your arms relaxed at your sides. Place your left foot on top of the bench. Contract your right calf and raise the heel off the floor as far as possible. Pause briefly, and then lower the heel again. Do all your repetitions with your right leg, then switch and repeat with your left.

Variation: You can perform the standing calf raise holding dumbbells at your sides or a medicine ball against your chest for added resistance.

SUPINE BRIDGE HEEL RAISE

(LIGHT, HEAVY)

Benefits: The supine bridge heel raise strengthens the calf muscles to produce a more powerful push-off in running. It also requires balance and core stabilization and thus enhances the stabilizing capacity of the abdominals, quadriceps, and gluteus maximus.

Procedure: Place your feet in a wide stance on the floor and rest your upper back, shoulders, and head on an exercise bench or other similar support (forming a "bridge" with your body). Pull your hips high so that your shins are at a right angle to the floor and your body is parallel to the floor from knees to neck. Contract your calf muscles and raise your heels off the floor as high as possible. Pause for 1 second, then return to the start position.

Variations: To increase the load component of this exercise, cross one leg over the other and perform a single-leg supine bridge heel raise. To increase the balance and core-stabilization component, use a stability ball instead of a bench or chair for support.

STRAIGHT-LEG HOP

(POWER)

Benefits: This exercise strengthens and increases the power of the calf muscles and enhances the ability to generate power in the push-off portion of the running stride.

Procedure: Stand with your feet close together and a medicine ball held straight overhead. Hop up and down on your toes while maintaining a slight bend in the knees. Push off with maximum force each time.

Variations: To make this exercise easier, hop without using a medicine ball. To make it more challenging, hop on one leg at a time.

LUNGE EXERCISES

The lunge portion of the running stride involves both legs, but in different roles. As one leg thrusts your body forward, using forceful contractions in all of the muscles on the back of the leg and involving the hip abductors for balance, the opposite leg swings forward and reaches out ahead of you. It uses primarily the muscles on the front of the thigh to straighten itself. The following lunge exercises simulate this action under load so that you can perform it with greater power and efficiency.

WALKING LUNGE
(LIGHT, HEAVY)

Benefits: The walking lunge strengthens the quadriceps, hip flexors, and hip extensors (hamstrings and buttocks). It helps to create a more powerful running stride and to correct muscular imbalances in the thigh musculature.

Procedure: Stand comfortably with your arms at your sides (or grasp one wrist with the opposite hand behind your back). Take a large step forward with your right leg, and bend the knee until your thigh is parallel to the floor. Thrust back upward and draw your left foot even with your right. Now lunge forward with the left leg.

Variation: You can perform the walking lunge using dumbbells (held at your sides) or a medicine ball (held straight in front of your chest) for added resistance.

SQUAT LEAP

(POWER)

Benefits: The squat leap increases the strength and power of the entire lower body and conditions the stabilizing muscles of the entire torso.

Procedure: Stand with one foot half a step ahead of the other and your knees bent slightly. Hold a medicine ball with your arms extended downward in front of your body. Using a steady, controlled motion, lower yourself into a deep squat, and then smoothly thrust upward into a full vertical leap while lifting your arms above your head. Make sure to maintain the natural arch in your spine throughout this movement.

As your feet leave the ground, point your toes, ensuring that your calves get involved. While elevated, reverse the position of your feet (move the forward foot half a step back and the rear foot half a step forward). Land on both feet and immediately lower your arms, bend your knees, and initiate the next deep squat.

Variation: To make this exercise easier, perform the squat leap without the medicine ball.

STEPUP

(LIGHT, HEAVY, POWER)

Benefits: The stepup strengthens the gluteals, hamstrings, and quadriceps and corrects muscular imbalance in the thigh muscles.

Procedure: Stand facing a 12- to 18-inch-high support platform (such as an exercise bench) about a step away from it while holding a dumbbell in each hand at your sides. Step up onto the bench with your left foot, and then push off your left heel as you raise your right leg so that you're standing on the bench. Step back down with your right leg. Continue stepping up and down, pushing with your left leg and carrying your right leg along for the ride, until you complete a full set, then switch legs and repeat with your right leg doing the work.

Variations: To perform a power version of this exercise, modify the procedure as follows. Step up with your left foot, and then drive your right thigh upward in an exaggerated running movement. Move your arms, too, as in running, and try to drive upward powerfully enough that your left foot lifts off the step slightly. When your left foot lands back on the step, lower your right foot back to the floor. When your right foot touches the floor, lift your left foot above the step a few inches and then drive it back downward (a skipping movement) to initiate another power stepup. After completing a full set of 10 to 15 repetitions with the left foot on the bench, switch to the right foot.

SIDE STEPUP

(LIGHT, HEAVY, POWER)

Benefits: The side stepup strengthens all the muscles between the waist and the knee. More than any other lunge exercise presented here, it strengthens the hip abductors (outer hip) and thereby helps prevent lateral pelvic tilting during running.

Procedure: Stand comfortably with a 12- to 18-inch-high support platform (such as an exercise bench) positioned to your right, about 6 inches from your foot. Use a lower platform if you're shorter and/or less advanced, a taller platform if you're taller and/or more advanced. Lift your right foot and place it on the bench. Press upward with your right leg until it's fully extended and your left foot is even with the right foot. Without allowing the left foot to rest on the bench, pause for 1 second in this position, then lower your left foot back to the floor. After completing a full set, switch legs.

Variations: For extra resistance, perform this exercise while holding a dumbbell in your outside hand (i.e., the hand opposite the foot on the bench). To do a power version of this exercise, modify the procedure as follows. When thrusting upward with the leg on the bench, follow through by pushing off with your toes so that your foot comes off the bench briefly. When your foot lands back on the bench, lower the other foot back to the floor without pausing. As soon as this foot touches the floor, lift the bench-supported foot off the bench a few inches (a skipping movement), and then drive it back downward to initiate the next power side stepup.

BENDING EXERCISES

The role that your lower back and abdominal muscles (known collectively as the core muscles) play in running may be subtler than the role played by your legs, but it's no less important. These muscles help you maintain proper posture and assist in the transfer of forces between your arms and legs. These bending exercises will allow your core muscles to do both jobs better.

GOOD MORNING
(LIGHT)

Benefits: The good morning strengthens the entire posterior side of the body from the hamstrings to the rear shoulders, but challenges the lower back above all. It helps improve running posture.

Procedure: Stand tall with your feet placed slightly farther than shoulder-width apart and your arms extended straight upward with a dumbbell in each hand. Bend forward at the hips (avoid rounding your back) and reach the dumbbells toward your toes, going as far as you can without bending your knees. Try to keep your arms more or less in line with your torso all the way down. Return slowly to the upright position, standing tall with arms overhead. Again, maintain a neutral spine.

Variation: Perform the good morning using a medicine ball for resistance. As you gain strength, switch to heavier balls or dumbbells.

STANDING MULTI-CRUNCH

(LIGHT, HEAVY, POWER)

Benefits: The standing multi-crunch strengthens the muscles of the abdomen, corrects muscular imbalance in the core musculature, and improves running posture.

Procedure: Attach a resistance band to a door at shoulder height. Face the point of attachment and hold the handles with your hands side-by-side and your arms outstretched. Step back until you have adequate tension in the band. Stand with your knees bent slightly. Bend forward at the hips with a curling motion of the spine. Bring the left handle outside and past your left knee and the right handle outside and past your right knee. Return smoothly to the start position.

Curl forward again, this time taking both arms to the outside of the right knee. Come back up to the starting position, and then curl to the left. That's 1 repetition.

TWISTING EXERCISES

MEDICINE-BALL TWIST
(LIGHT)

Benefits: The medicine-ball twist strengthens the obliques for better torso stability during running.

Procedure: Stand with your feet shoulder-width apart and your knees bent slightly. Hold a medicine ball with your arms extended straight in front of your chest. Keeping your hips locked, twist to the left as far as you can comfortably go, then slowly twist all the way to the right. Don't pause at the start position in either direction. Make sure to do this exercise slowly, because if you build up too much momentum, you could hurt your back as you change the direction of your rotation.

Variation: Perform this exercise using a dumbbell for resistance instead of a medicine ball. Hold the dumbbell vertically with both hands.

RESISTANCE-BAND TWIST

(LIGHT, HEAVY, POWER)

Benefits: The resistance-band twist strengthens the obliques for better torso stability during running.

Procedure: Attach a resistance band to a door at shoulder height. Stand with your left side facing the door while grasping a handle in both hands. The farther you are from the door, the more tension you'll have in the band. Begin with your arms fully extended in front of your chest and your trunk rotated to the left (toward the door). Twist smoothly to the right as far as you can comfortably go, keeping your hands straight in front of the center of your chest. Pause briefly, then return to the start position. After completing a full set of 8 to 20 repetitions (depending on workout type), turn around and twist to the left.

PUSHING AND PULLING EXERCISES

The muscles of the shoulders and upper back produce the arm-swing portion of the running stride. In order to do this job well, they need not have tremendous raw power, but they do need to generate force economically—that is, with minimal energy. These pushing and pulling exercises will improve the efficiency of your arm swing.

BALANCING RESISTANCE-BAND CHEST PRESS

(LIGHT, HEAVY, POWER)

Benefits: The balancing resistance-band chest press strengthens the pushing muscles of the chest for a more powerful arm action during running and strengthens the stabilizing muscles of the torso for better control of lateral forces during running.

Procedure: Attach a resistance band to a door frame at shoulder height. Grab a handle in each hand, and stand with your back to the door frame. Standing farther away from the door will increase the amount of tension on the band. Begin with your hands positioned palms down, right in front of your armpits. Lift your right foot off the floor and throw a smooth, controlled forward punch with your left arm, twisting slightly at the waist in order to maximize your reach. Slowly retract your arm toward your armpit and return your right foot to the floor. Now lift your left foot and throw a punch with the right hand.

BENT-OVER ROW

(LIGHT, HEAVY, POWER)

Benefits: The bent-over row strengthens the muscles of the upper back to produce a more powerful arm action during running.

Procedure: Stand with your left foot one big step ahead of your right. Bend both knees moderately and lean forward about 30 degrees from the waist. Brace your left hand on your lower left thigh. Grasp a dumbbell in your right hand and begin with your right arm fully extended toward the floor. Pull the dumbbell toward a spot just outside your lower ribcage, keeping your elbow in. Slowly lower the dumbbell. After completing a full set, reverse your stance and switch arms.

Variation: Use a resistance band instead of a dumbbell for resistance. Stand on the band with your forward foot while pulling on a handle with the opposite hand.

DUMBBELL RUNNING

(LIGHT)

Benefits: Dumbbell running strengthens the front and rear shoulders and enhances the ability to generate power in the arm-swing portion of the running motion.

Procedure: Assume a split stance with your left foot flat on the floor and one step ahead of your right foot. Grab a pair of light dumbbells and perform a smooth and controlled running motion with your arms, keeping your elbows bent at 90 degrees. Continue for 30 to 60 seconds, then reverse your stance and repeat.

INTEGRATED EXERCISES

Integrated exercises are those that combine two or more of the component movements of the running stride. Their advantages are that they are more functional for runners than any single-component exercise and that they are potential time-savers. However, they are less likely to produce as pronounced a training effect in any given component as another exercise that isolates that movement. For this reason, I recommend that you regularly incorporate the following exercises into your strength program, but do not make them the basis of the program.

SIDE LUNGE AND REACH

(LIGHT, HEAVY)

Benefits: The side lunge and reach strengthens the hamstrings, quadriceps, and hip abductors and adductors. It improves the stability of the pelvis and lower back and enhances the transfer of forces between the legs and upper body.

Procedure: Stand tall with your feet placed shoulder-width apart and your arms relaxed at your sides, a light dumbbell in each hand. Take a large step to the left with your left foot, and bend the left knee deeply. At the same time, reach with both dumbbells toward a spot on the floor slightly outside your left toe. Bend at the hips and avoid rounding the back. Push back powerfully with your left leg to return to the start position. Now lunge with the right leg.

Variation: Perform the side lunge and reach while holding a medicine ball.

TWO-ARM TWIST

(LIGHT, HEAVY, POWER)

Benefits: The two-arm twist combines twist, bend, and lunge movements to create a true total-body exercise. It's especially beneficial in enhancing the transfer of forces between the legs and upper body.

Procedure: Attach a resistance band to the bottom of a door. Stand in a wide stance with your left side facing the door and most of your weight on your left foot. Grasp a handle in both hands, beginning with the handle just outside your lower left shin. Using both arms, pull the band upward and across your body, finishing above your right shoulder. Avoid rounding your back. Return smoothly to the start position. After completing a full set, switch sides.

Variation: Attach the resistance band to the door at head height and pull it from high to low.

SINGLE-ARM PULL

(LIGHT, HEAVY, POWER)

Benefits: The single-arm pull integrates pull and twist movements. It strengthens the upper-body muscles used during running and enhances control over lateral forces when running.

Procedure: Attach the band to a door, slightly above shoulder height. Stand in a split stance, facing the door, with your right foot forward and most of your weight on your right foot. Hold the handle in your right hand at full forward reach. Pull the handle toward your armpit, twisting your trunk to the right as you go. As you retract the right arm, reach forward with the left. After completing a full set while pulling with your right arm, switch arms and legs so that your left foot is forward and you pull with your left hand.

SINGLE-LEG SQUAT

(LIGHT)

Benefits: The single-leg squat integrates lunge and bend movements. It strengthens the hip extensors (hamstrings and gluteals) and lower back. It enhances pelvic stability during running, improves running posture and the transfer of forces between the upper body and legs, and yields a more powerful running stride.

Procedure: Stand on your right foot with your left knee slightly bent and your left foot elevated an inch or two above the floor. Bend your right leg and reach with your left hand toward a spot on the floor located 10 to 16 inches in front of your right foot. Your right arm and left leg will naturally reach behind your body for balance. Return to the start position. Do a full set and then repeat with your left foot planted.

Variation: For added challenge, perform this exercise with a dumbbell in your reaching hand or with dumbbells in both hands.

CORRECTIVE EXERCISES
FOR THE LOWER-LEG STABILIZERS

If you could choose only one muscle area to strengthen, it would have to be your shin muscles, those that pull your toes up toward your knee, thus performing the opposite function of your calf muscles. Strengthening them will stabilize your ankles, will reduce strain on your calf muscles during running, and can help to correct overpronation, thus preventing many running injuries. It will also increase your running efficiency by lessening ground contact time and increasing the amount of force that returns to your foot from the ground.

Some of these exercises (the middle three) strengthen muscles in the foot as well as muscles in the shin. Though small, the foot muscles do quite a bit of work during the contact phase of the running stride. When these muscles are strong, they get your foot back off the ground more quickly and are able to push off more powerfully. They're worth some attention.

TOE DIP

Stand on a block or sturdy box with your forefeet hanging over the edge. Brace your hands against a wall for support. Lower your toes toward the floor as far as comfortably possible, and then lift them again. Repeat for 30 seconds.

PILLOW BALANCING

Place a pillow on the floor and balance on it with one shoeless foot for 30 seconds, then balance on the other foot. At first it'll be difficult to last 30 seconds, but you'll quickly improve. Keep it challenging by using a bigger or softer pillow, by stacking pillows, and/or by balancing longer.

TOWEL SCRUNCH

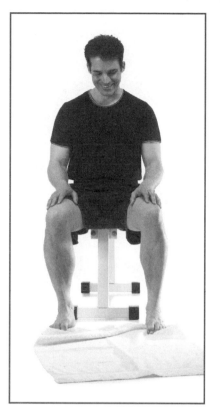

Sit in a chair with your feet flat on the floor and a towel laid out just in front of your toes. Use the toes of both feet to pull (or "scrunch") the towel underneath your feet bit by bit. Pull once with the left foot, then once with the right, and repeat until you can't scrunch any more of the towel. This is much easier on a wood or tile floor than on carpet.

PICKING UP MARBLES

Sit in a chair, and use the toes of both feet to pick up marbles from the floor and drop them down again. Do this for a few minutes.

TRACING THE ALPHABET

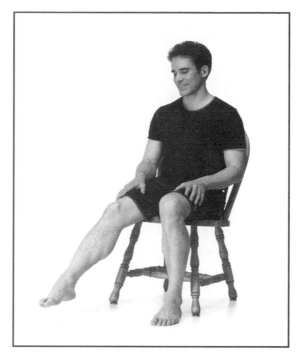

While sitting in a chair, lift your right foot a few inches above the floor and trace each letter of the alphabet in the air, as though your big toe were a piece of chalk. After you trace Z, switch to the left foot.

GET WITH THE PROGRAM

You now have a good selection of corrective and functional strength exercises at your disposal. It's time to create an actual strength program from these exercises.

As I said earlier in the chapter, there are three different types of strength workouts you should do: light, heavy, and power. Each has a slightly different effect on your body. A light workout increases the muscles' endurance; a heavy workout increases their maximum strength; and a power workout increases—what else?—their power, which is a combination of strength and speed.

Each workout should include one exercise representing each of the six exercise types I've shown you: plantar flexion, lunge, bend, twist, push and/or pull, and a corrective exercise for the lower-leg stabilizers. If you include integrated exercises, you can lessen the total number of exercises you perform. For example, the single-leg squat counts as both a lunge and a bend.

If you include a push exercise, such as the resistance-band chest press, be sure to also do a pull in the same workout or the next one. Also, be aware that some bending exercises, such as the standing multi-crunch, challenge the abdominals but not the spinal erectors, while others, such as the good morning, do the opposite. So be sure to balance these as well.

As noted earlier, corrective exercises for the lower legs do not have light, heavy, and power versions; perform these the same way each time.

As you can see from the workout descriptions, you can use many of these exercises in more than one of the three workout types. What distinguishes light, heavy, and power workouts is not so much the exercises as the degree of resistance, the number of repetitions per set, and the speed at which each repetition is performed. Here are guidelines for each workout type.

LIGHT WORKOUT

In a light workout, perform one or more sets of 15 to 20 repetitions of each exercise at a moderate tempo—that is, a speed that feels natural for the movement, not deliberately slow and not rushed. You never want to go to "failure" on a light day. In other words, you want to make sure that at the end of each set of each exercise, you have something left in the tank—you could've done 2 more repetitions, but you chose not to. So choose the weight or resistance you use accordingly.

In the case of body-weight exercises (such as walking lunges), in which changing the resistance is impossible, just do 2 fewer repetitions than the most you could do with perfect form, up to a maximum of 25 repetitions. Another exception is dumbbell running, which you should perform by time—30 to 60 seconds with the left foot forward and 30 to 60 seconds more with the right foot forward. Do one to three sets of each exercise in circuit fashion (in other words, do a set of every exercise before you do a second set of any of them). Rest for 30 to 45 seconds between sets.

HEAVY WORKOUT

In a heavy workout, do 8 to 10 repetitions of each exercise at a slow, or at least deliberate, speed. Once again, you don't want to go to "failure." Stop each set 1 repetition short of the point at which you couldn't do any more with perfect form.

In the case of body-weight exercises, just do 1 less repetition than the most you could do with perfect form, up to a maximum of 15 repetitions. (If you can do more than 15, choose a harder exercise.) Do one to three sets, and again do the routine as a circuit. Rest for 60 to 90 seconds between sets.

POWER WORKOUT

In a power workout, do 10 to 15 repetitions of each exercise that involves a form of resistance other than body weight at a fast tempo. Choose a resistance you could lift once or twice more (at a fast tempo) than you actually do. Repeat all body-weight power exercises (e.g., straight-leg hop) for up to 1 minute. Be sure to choose exercises that you can perform safely at a fast tempo. Rest for 45 to 60 seconds between sets.

In order to create a year-round strength-training regimen using these workouts, simply cycle through the three workout types repetitively with a frequency of two or three strength workouts per week. (Two workouts are plenty; three is the limit.) You may wish to do more frequent and perhaps also longer strength workouts (two or three complete circuits) in the winter to build a reserve of strength, and then do fewer and possibly shorter strength workouts (one or two circuits) during the remainder of the year to maintain strength and prevent injuries.

Here are a few more tips.

- **If you've never strength-trained or if you have not done so in a while, perform only light workouts for 4 weeks before mixing in heavy and power workouts, and start with just one circuit.**

- **On days when you plan to run and strength-train, try to do the run first if you're planning to go long or hard, but feel free to do them in either order otherwise.**

- **Don't perform any strength workouts in the week before an important race.**

STRENGTH-BUILDING RUNNING DRILLS

Running itself is a form of strength exercise that involves body-weight resistance. You can improve your stride power only so much by running normally. However, by modifying the circumstances of normal running just slightly, you can perform drills that serve as functional strength exercises for running within the discipline of running itself. Following are four such drills. Performing two or more of these drills weekly will provide a fitness "bridge" that serves to maximize the functional transfer of the strength you gain in your strength workouts over to your normal running.

HIGH KNEES. Run in place or slowly forward for 30 seconds with exaggerated knee lift, bringing your thigh up parallel to the ground with each stride. Keep your torso erect.

BUTT KICKS. Run slowly forward for 30 seconds with very limited movement of your thighs (tiny steps) and highly exaggerated foot lift behind your body (as though you're trying to kick yourself in the butt with your heels).

HILL STRIDES. After completing a normal training run, find a moderately steep hill and run up it for 20 seconds at your 1-mile race pace with slightly exaggerated form (longer strides than normal and more arm swing). Jog slowly back down, and repeat three to five times.

BOUNDING. After completing a normal training run, find a soft, flat surface such as a soccer field and "bound" for 20 seconds—that is, run with highly exaggerated forward and vertical displacement and arm swing. Jog slowly back to your starting point and repeat three times.

THREE

FLEXIBILITY TRAINING

BELIEVE IT OR NOT, stretching is one of the most controversial subjects in exercise and sport. For many years, experts, would-be experts, athletes, and coaches have disagreed about:

- Whether stretching prevents injuries, causes injuries, or does neither

- Whether stretching enhances athletic performance, hinders it, or has no effect either way

- When and how often one should stretch, if ever

- Perhaps most important, how a muscle ought to be stretched, if it's going to be stretched at all

I wish I could tell you that all of these issues have been resolved, but they haven't. Nevertheless, based on extensive research and personal experience, I'll say with complete confidence that every runner should stretch regularly, and I'm going to recommend some reliable guidelines for doing so. I can also assure you that *appropriate* stretching practices will never cause an injury and may prevent and rehabilitate many.

However, because stretching for sports remains an inexact science, some of these guidelines are relatively loose, and I'll give you options to choose from. Specifically, I will present four distinct types of flexibility training—static, active-isolated (AI), contract-relax (CR), and yoga—and leave it to you to decide which method or combination of methods you will use.

In terms of frequency and volume of stretching, I'll give you recommended minimums but leave open the options of stretching more often and of doing a greater variety of stretches than the minimum. I'll also refrain from pretending that any absolute laws exist regarding when you should stretch: before runs, after runs, before and after runs, or at other times of day far removed from your runs.

Your body will have the final say as to which flexibility training practices work best for you. None of the options I suggest will harm you, but I can't guarantee that all of them will work equally well for every runner. In this regard, flexibility work is a lot like other aspects of training: Each athlete is an experiment of one.

THE FLEXIBILITY NEEDS OF RUNNERS

Stretching advocates frequently promote the idea that the more flexible your joints are, the better you will perform in all sports. This is simply not true. Flexibility needs differ widely from one sport to another, and there is such a thing as excessive flexibility in most types of athlete, runners included. In one study, a group of elite runners was tested for both hamstring flexibility and running economy. Those with the *least* flexible hamstrings had the greatest economy. The study concluded that the runners with tighter hamstrings probably had more stable knee joints. Thus, in theory, they used less energy per stride than runners with more wobbly knees.

Interesting, to be sure, but you can't look at a study of elite runners and assume the findings apply to you. If I were to make a generalization about the average runner, I'd say you're more likely to be held back by hamstrings that are too tight than hampered by hamstrings that are too loose. Still, I think I've made my point that flexibility is not a case of "the more, the better." A runner requires sufficient range of motion to take long, powerful strides. Any extra range of motion will provide no additional benefit and will more likely reduce energy economy.

There are two distinct types of flexibility, only one of which really matters to runners. Passive flexibility refers to the extreme limits of a joint's range of motion (ROM) when an outside force—a person or object—is used to position the limb or limb segment. A good example is the full front split, since you're using the floor to help your legs get into

ROLE MODEL
CATHY O'BRIEN

New Hampshire's seacoast region was a small hotbed of running fame in the late 1980s, when I was touring its back roads daily as a teenage runner. The girls' cross-country and track coach at my high school in the town of Durham was none other than Jeff Johnson, the man who named Nike and created many of the company's early running shoes. One town over, in Newmarket, lived Lynn Jennings, who would win three consecutive World Cross-Country Championships beginning the year after my graduation. And one town over on the other side, in Dover, was Cathy Schiro (soon to become Cathy O'Brien), who had brought glory to the area by winning the 1984 High School National Cross-Country Championship.

O'Brien brought a lot more glory to the area over the next dozen years. She competed in the 1988 and 1992 Olympic marathons, finishing 10th in the latter. She set a world record for 10 miles (51:47) in 1989 and was the top-ranked American road racer the following year. In 1991, she won the Los Angeles Marathon in a career-best time of 2:29:30. She also won the 15-K National Championship in 1995. Now a mother of two, O'Brien still runs competitively and still lives in my old hometown.

The real reason I'm talking about Cathy O'Brien is that she was among the first elite runners to begin dabbling in yoga. Like many runners, she was always rather inflexible. Yoga helped her loosen up, but its greatest benefit, she has said, was the relaxation response that it induced, along with the sheer enjoyment of holding its preternaturally satisfying poses.

O'Brien also enjoys swimming, which she has done when injured to maintain cardiovascular fitness, and with good results. Her strength-training regimen includes calisthenics and leg exercises using a resistance band.

this position. The ability to do a split demonstrates a high degree of passive flexibility in your hip joints. Dynamic flexibility, on the other hand, refers to how far a given limb is able to move by its own force. A leaping full front split demonstrates a high degree of dynamic flexibility in your hip joints, because your legs must achieve the split position without assistance from any outside force.

Passive flexibility comes mostly from elasticity in the connective tissues surrounding your joints. Dynamic flexibility, by contrast, comes from a combination of elasticity in the connective tissues and *strength* in the muscles that create joint actions. Put another way, passive flexibility is range of motion, plain and simple. Dynamic flexibility is strength throughout the range of motion. There is some degree of overlap between the two types of flexibility, but they are distinct.

What matters to runners is dynamic, not passive, flexibility, because when you run, each leg moves itself. Consider the still-action photographs you've seen depicting elite runners in full stride. The toe of the trailing leg is just coming off the ground behind the runner. This trailing leg is extended quite a ways behind the runner; the thigh is a good 45 degrees beyond vertical in that direction. The forward leg, meanwhile, is sharply bent, the knee high in front of the runner. What you're seeing in such images is excellent dynamic range of motion in the striding movement.

Slower runners look quite different. They tend to shuffle, even when running very hard. They don't achieve the same rear extension with the push-off leg or the same knee lift with the forward leg. This is because they lack elasticity in the muscles that are required to relax and stretch (the antagonists), and possibly also strength in the muscles that contract (the agonists) in the striding movement.

Through flexibility training, runners can increase their dynamic flexibility and stride length. While flexibility training is generally considered to be synonymous with stretching, the best way to increase dynamic flexibility is to combine stretching with strength training. Stretching primarily increases range of motion, while strength training primarily increases strength throughout the range of motion.

So the way I've separated strength training from flexibility training in the structure of this book is a somewhat artificial convenience. In fact, stretching and strength training very often happen simultaneously. Whenever you move a joint, muscles on one side of it contract while muscles on the other side relax and stretch. Picture a simple strength exercise, the biceps curl (simple, and functionally useless for runners). The biceps, on the front of your arm, contract as you curl the weight toward your shoulders. The triceps, on the back of your arm, relax and stretch.

Two types of stretching—AI and CR—use this principle to great advantage. You contract one set of muscles, achieving a mild strengthening effect, before you stretch the opposite set of muscles, improving dynamic flexibility. On the other hand, many functional strength-training exercises take the muscles through a full range of motion and therefore serve as a perfect complement to stretching. Strength training does, of course, tend to develop the strength aspect of dynamic flexibility more than stretching will, whereas the latter tends to increase range of motion more, so both are needed.

As I mentioned in the previous chapter on strength training, running tends to reduce the elasticity of certain muscles, resulting in muscular imbalances that frequently cause overuse injuries. So runners need to train for flexibility not just to increase muscle elasticity and thereby improve their performance but also to prevent these same muscles from becoming less elastic. The same methods accomplish both jobs.

One final note: Consistent flexibility training is especially important for masters runners, because muscles gradually lose elasticity with aging.

GUIDELINES FOR FLEXIBILITY TRAINING

Stretching before a run is usually neither necessary nor beneficial. An easy jogging warmup, by itself, will loosen up your running muscles enough to allow them to perform effectively and without straining.

Having said this, I do recommend that you stretch right before the high-intensity portions of your workouts. Most acute hamstring strains and calf-muscle pulls befall runners during speed workouts, when they're taking their longest and most forceful strides. A simple warmup jog may not prepare your muscles to safely handle such a test. And if you're dealing with an existing injury—a mild muscle pull or strain, for example—you should stretch the affected muscle after every warmup, whether or not high-intensity work follows.

In those cases, choose an appropriate static, AI, or CR stretch from the selection presented later in this chapter, and perform it following 5 or more minutes of walking or easy running. (Yoga poses don't make the best warmup stretches; they aren't as functional for runners, and in some cases they require their own warmup—stretches to prepare you for stretches.)

The best stretches to do before high-intensity running are those that increase your main running muscles' active range of motion from a resting level to a level that's appropriate for fast running. After a gentle warmup run lasting at least 5 minutes, perform the following three drills in the order presented.

WARMUP DRILLS

HIGH KNEES. Run in place for 20 seconds. Bring your thighs up parallel to the ground with each stride. In addition to building strength, as described in the previous chapter, this drill increases the active ROM of the hamstrings and calves. It also elevates the heart rate and warms, lubricates, and shunts extra blood to the leg muscles, preparing them for sustained running.

GIANT STEPS. Walk about 50 meters by taking giant lunge steps. You should achieve a 90-degree bend in the forward leg before pushing off with the toes and taking a subsequent giant step with the trailing leg. This drill increases the active ROM of the hip flexors, hamstrings, and calves.

SKIPPING. Skip 50 meters at a brisk but controlled pace. Begin by bringing one leg up to the point where the thigh is parallel to the ground, as in the high knees drill. When this leg is at peak height, take a small hop-step forward with the opposite foot. Lower the striding foot to the ground a step ahead of the hopping foot, and then stride with the second leg. Move your arms in opposition to your legs as you would when running normally. This drill increases the active ROM of the calves and hamstrings.

The ideal time to stretch is immediately after running or any endurance cross-training. The muscles are warm and well-lubricated, and therefore prepared to stretch without straining (as long as you stretch properly). It's also easiest to counteract the muscle-tightening effect of running when you stretch regularly following training sessions.

Stretching right after a workout may also accelerate the muscle-recovery process by keeping bloodflow elevated, thereby speeding the delivery of nutrients (especially amino acids, needed for tissue repair) and the removal of metabolic wastes. You may even feel the benefit in the form of reduced postworkout muscle soreness. While clinical investigations of the link between postexercise stretching and muscle soreness have produced mixed results, in my experience (and in that of countless other runners), there is a clear positive connection. I definitely experience less muscle soreness and stiffness when I stretch regularly following workouts than when I do not. Stretching after strength training works the same magic for me.

You can also stretch at other times: while watching a ballgame on TV on a weekend afternoon, before going to bed, at work, whenever. But when you do stretch at times that are completely separate from your workouts, you have to remember that your muscles are cold and simply won't have the same range of motion they'll have when fully warm. This is okay—there's really nothing wrong with stretching cold muscles. Your body can deal with it. You just have to ease into it very gradually. Your muscles won't necessarily warm up while you're stretching—in fact, their internal temperature may go down a bit—but your muscles and connective tissues can still get the message and can lengthen without injuring themselves.

On the other hand, if you stretch them too far too quickly—whether they're warm or cold—you'll create injuries within muscle fibers and connective tissues. You don't need me to tell you that's two steps backward, in place of the intended step forward.

Is there a bad time to stretch? I can think of two: one fixed, one situational.

I think it's a terrible idea to stretch first thing in the morning, right when you get out of bed. Your spinal discs fill up with fluid overnight, when you're horizontal, and are much more prone to injury when you first wake up. (For that reason, first-thing-in-the-morning strength training can be a hazard, too, if you neglect a thorough warmup.) After you've been vertical for an hour or two, your discs should be lighter and less vulnerable.

I also recommend extreme caution when you stretch strained or pulled muscles. If the injury is mild, gentle stretching will help the muscle heal at a functional length and may also help minimize scar-tissue formation. If gentle stretching is painful, leave the muscle be until you can stretch it without pain. Try massaging it instead.

As for how often you should stretch, three times a week should be considered a minimum. If you stretch any less, it's doubtful that you'll be able to prevent the tightening of muscles such as the hamstrings and gastrocnemius that results from frequent running, let alone increase your dynamic flexibility. Once-daily stretching is more or less the perfect amount for most muscle groups in most runners. But if you have a "problem area" that is extremely tight and hindering performance or perhaps teetering on the brink of injury, twice-daily stretching may be in order.

The most important muscles to stretch are the hamstrings, gastrocnemius, soleus, and hip flexors. Two tendons, the iliotibial band and the Achilles, deserve equal attention. Your stretching routine should cover these muscles and tendons at least, and you should always stretch them the most. Of secondary importance are the lower back, piriformis (located deep within the buttock), hip abductors and adductors, and quadriceps. (Refer back to the muscle illustrations in chapter 2 for the locations of these important muscles.) I strongly advise you to stretch these muscles regularly, too, but if you're stubborn, then stretch the first group for now and add the second group once you've learned to love flexibility training. (It really is a very pleasant activity once you've made it a habit.) There's some benefit to stretching the muscles of the trunk as well, especially for those with postural irregularities (which is most of us). I do so twice a week. Nor is there any harm in stretching the rest of your body—shoulders, chest, neck, arms, hands, and feet. However, I don't include stretches for all of these areas in this chapter.

You increase dynamic flexibility much the same way you gain strength and build endurance. Think "incremental gains" rather than "instant results." Pushing your stretches hard from the first day makes about as much sense as running 22 miles on your first day of marathon training. The best advice I can offer is to ease into it, be patient, and enjoy making progress step-by-step.

FOUR WAYS TO STRETCH

STATIC. Of the four types of stretching I mentioned at the start of this chapter—static, AI, CR, and yoga—the first is the simplest and most popular. The standard toe touch is an example of a static stretch.

Static stretches are usually facilitated, meaning that the targeted muscles don't stretch themselves. They're stretched by the work of other muscles. Take that basic toe touch, for example. The hamstrings don't stretch themselves, and the opposing muscles, the quadriceps on the front of the thigh, don't really do anything either. Rather, the stretch happens because your pelvis tilts forward.

Most of the time, you'll hold static stretches for 10 to 30 seconds. Two repetitions seem to work better than 1, unless you hold the first stretch long enough for the muscle to relax and then go into a deeper stretch from that point.

Static stretching generally gets high marks in scientific research; it definitely improves your passive range of motion. Whether it increases dynamic range of motion is open to debate and likely depends on the other training activities you do. For example, static stretching combined with functional strength training is probably a good way to get improvements in passive and dynamic range of motion.

The biggest criticism of static stretching comes from those who advocate AI and CR. They contend that if you hold a stretch longer than a second or two, a protective reflex causes the muscle to contract and shorten in order to prevent overstretching and, thus, injury. According to that point of view, static stretches attempt the impossible: lengthening a muscle while it's fighting to shorten itself. At best, this makes the effort useless, from a functional point of view. At worst, it could lead to injury.

Research doesn't exactly back up this argument, however. Static stretching seems to improve passive range of motion at least as well as AI does. And as mentioned above, you can teach your body to relax into a deeper stretch, thus circumventing the muscle-tightening stretch reflex. The mechanism at work is called the inverted stretch reflex, which causes a muscle to go with the flow of a prolonged stretch. You can learn to use it, but it takes some practice and focus. You have to concentrate on relaxing the targeted muscles throughout the stretch, something few athletes will do.

A second limitation of static stretching is that few traditional stretches successfully isolate individual muscle groups. While muscle isolation is not desirable in strength training, it is generally preferable in flexibility training, because the more muscles share a stretch, the less each muscle is stretched. The toe touch stretches not just the hamstrings but also the buttocks and lower back. If you straighten your knees completely, it also tugs on your calf muscles. The AI and CR methods have more ways to stretch individual muscles, making a hamstring stretch truly a hamstring stretch. Still, static stretching is the simplest form of stretching and is demonstrably effective.

ACTIVE-ISOLATED. Active-isolated stretching is a form of flexibility training that was created specifically to overcome the drawbacks of static stretching. In an AI stretch, you put your body in a position that allows you to stretch a single muscle group. Then you contract the muscles *opposite* the ones you want to stretch while pulling the targeted muscles into a deeper stretch than would ordinarily be possible. For example, you'd contract your quadriceps while stretching your hamstrings. Each stretch lasts 2 seconds and is usually performed in sets of 10 repetitions.

Most AI stretches require a rope to help you pull the muscles into deeper stretches. The major limitation of the method is that some of the stretches are rather awkward and simply don't feel like they're doing much.

AI stretching was originally developed as an assisted stretching method; a partner (or in some cases one's own hand or hands) served in place of the rope. While I've never had a partner help me perform AI stretches, I'm certain that some of the stretches would be much more effective if I did have one. For example, I no longer perform AI stretches for my calves, because I get a better feeling and, I think, better results from static stretches for the calves.

CONTRACT-RELAX. Contract-relax stretches are similar to AI. Both entail isolation of a single, targeted muscle group via briefly held stretches. In CR stretching, however, you precede each stretch with an isometric contraction of the targeted muscle. So if you're stretching your hamstrings, you first contract them, then relax and stretch them. This helps trigger the inverted stretch reflex. CR has scored high marks as a flexibility-training tool in studies. But like certain AI stretches, a few CR stretches would seem to be more effective if assisted by a partner.

YOGA. Yoga involves static-active stretching, making it a hybrid of the other forms of stretching I've just described. As in static stretching (whose proper technical name is static-passive stretching), you assume and hold positions in which certain muscles are lengthened. Like CR, yoga also involves isometric contractions, but with a crucial difference: In CR, you contract and relax the same muscle in a coordinated sequence; in yoga, you hold one set of muscles in isometric contractions while relaxing and stretching the muscles opposite them.

Yoga is seen by many as a complete form of exercise. It increases passive and dynamic flexibility as well as balance and coordination, which seems obvious. Some new research shows it also has strong, and nearly instant, powers to alleviate anxiety and stress.

It's also thought to improve strength, depending on the type of yoga practiced. For example, power yoga, in which you move quickly from one pose to the next, probably improves strength, particularly if you aren't performing any other type of strength training. Because it involves sustained isometric muscle contractions, yoga is a lot more taxing than other forms of flexibility training.

I made the mistake of trying my first yoga class within 3 weeks before racing a marathon. Unaccustomed to the type of physical challenge imposed by yoga, I found myself barely able to move the next day and sore for another 3 days. It spoiled my running for more than half a week—a crucial week. The lesson: Yoga is challenging; approach it accordingly. If you've never done it, I recommend that you try it during the off-season or the early portion of the base phase of the training cycle, beginning slowly.

In addition to the yoga poses demonstrated in this chapter, you can learn many other poses from books, videos, and classes. In any case, I strongly recommend that a beginner take at least a few classes led by a professional instructor, because it's very difficult to perform many of the poses properly at first, and without supervision it's equally difficult to know exactly what you might be doing improperly.

The following pages provide examples of each of the four types of stretching. I encourage you to experiment with the various stretching methods. This is the best way to ensure that you wind up doing the best stretch for each muscle group. If you happen to like, say, all of the CR stretches best, so be it; but if you find that you feel best when you supplement these with yoga stretches or when you substitute in a couple of static stretches, there's no reason not to go ahead and do so.

STATIC STRETCHES

CHEST AND SHOULDERS

Lace the fingers of both hands together behind your buttocks with your arms fully extended. Now rotate your arms gently upward until you feel a stretch in your chest and in the front of your shoulders. Hold for 20 seconds, relax, and repeat.

UPPER BACK

Lace the fingers of both hands together and extend your arms in front of your chest so that your arms and shoulders form a circle. Now shrug your shoulders upward and forward. You should feel a stretch in the rear of your shoulders and your upper back. Hold this stretch for 10 seconds and then lean to the left. The stretch will migrate into the large muscles on the right side of your back. Hold for 10 seconds, then lean to the right and stretch the left side of your back for another 10 seconds. Repeat the entire sequence.

LOWER BACK

Sit on the floor with both legs sharply bent and both heels resting on the floor, feet shoulder-width apart. Reach between your legs with both arms and rest your hands on the floor. Begin with your trunk upright. By contracting your abdominal muscles, tilt your trunk toward the floor as far as you can. Tuck your chin toward your chest as you begin the movement. As you near the limit of your range of motion, grab your lower shins or the bottoms of your feet with your hands, and extend the movement slightly with a gentle pull. Hold for 20 seconds, relax, and repeat.

GLUTES AND HIP ABDUCTORS

Lie on your back with your right arm extended away from your body and resting palm down on the floor. Bend your right leg 90 degrees, and reach the knee across your body and toward the floor outside your left hip. Make sure your right shoulder blade maintains contact with the floor. Use pressure from your left hand to enhance the stretch. Hold the stretch for 15 to 20 seconds, and then stretch your left side. Repeat on both sides.

HIP FLEXORS

Kneel on your left knee and place your right foot flat on the floor well in front of your body. Draw your navel toward your spine. Now put your weight forward into the lunge until you feel a good stretch in the front of your left hip. Hold the stretch for 20 seconds, and then repeat with your left foot forward, stretching your right-side hip flexors. Repeat on both sides.

HIP ADDUCTORS

Perform this one just as you would the hip-flexor stretch on the opposite page, but start with your forward foot angled out 45 degrees instead of straight ahead. Again, hold the stretch for 20 seconds, and then stretch the opposite side. Repeat on both sides.

HAMSTRINGS

Sit with your right leg outstretched in front of you. Splay your left knee wide and tuck the foot against the inside of your right thigh. (This is often called a figure-four stretch, because your legs form that numeral.) Bend forward from the hips, and grasp the shin of your right leg as close to the foot as you can. Don't round your back; that'll increase your reach but actually take emphasis off your hamstrings, making the stretch less effective. Hold the stretch for 10 to 15 seconds, and then stretch your left leg. Repeat on both sides.

ILIOTIBIAL BAND

Lie on your left side with your left leg slightly bent and your right leg bent fully. Grasp the top of your right foot with your right hand. Pull your foot back as you reach toward the floor with your knee so that your thigh simultaneously moves backward and rotates internally. You should feel a stretch along the outside of your thigh. Hold this stretch for 20 seconds, and then switch to your right side and stretch the left leg. Repeat on both sides.

QUADRICEPS

Stand on one foot and rest the top of the other foot on a desk-height object behind you. The thigh of this leg should be perpendicular to the floor. Rest your hands
on your hips. Rotate your pelvis backward. Hold the stretch for 10 to 15 seconds,
and then stretch the opposite leg. Now repeat the stretch on both sides.

GASTROCNEMIUS AND SOLEUS

Brace your hands against a wall and extend one leg far enough behind you that you feel a good stretch in your calf when you place the foot flat on the ground. Hold for 10 to 12 seconds, and then bend the knee slightly so that the stretch migrates from your gastrocnemius to your soleus. Hold for 10 seconds, and then stretch the opposite leg. Repeat the entire sequence.

ACHILLES TENDON

Stand in a split stance, one foot a step ahead of the other, with both feet flat on the ground and both knees slightly bent. Bend your back leg a little more and concentrate on trying to "sink" your butt straight down toward the heel of that foot. Keep your torso upright. You should begin to feel a stretch in your Achilles tendon. You may have to fiddle with your position before you find it. When you do, hold for 10 to 12 seconds, relax, and then stretch the opposite leg. Repeat on both sides.

ACTIVE-ISOLATED STRETCHES

NECK

Lace together the fingers of both hands and place them against the back of your head. Tip your head forward as far as comfortably possible and extend the movement slightly with gentle pressure from your hands. Pause for 1 second and relax. Perform 10 repetitions. Then place just the right hand on the left side of your head. Tilt your head to the right as far as comfortably possible, pause, relax, and repeat 9 times. Stretch the right side of your neck in the same way by using your left hand.

SHOULDER ROTATORS

Raise your arms into a "Don't shoot!" position—upper arms forming a straight line with your shoulders, forearms vertical. Now contract the muscles of your rear shoulders and squeeze your shoulder blades together so that your arms move backward several inches. At the limit of this small movement, pause briefly, relax, and repeat. Perform 10 repetitions and then invert your position so that your forearms are extended directly toward the floor and your palms face backward. Again, squeeze your shoulder blades together 10 times.

LOWER BACK

Lie on your back, bend both knees, and begin with your feet flat on the floor. Place your hands on your hamstrings just above your knees. Pull your knees as close to your chest as possible by contracting your stomach muscles and hip flexors. Gently assist the movement with pressure from your hands. Hold for 2 seconds, then lower your legs. Do 10 repetitions.

BENT-LEG HAMSTRINGS

Lie on your back with both legs bent. Begin with your left foot flat on the floor and your right leg elevated so that the thigh is perpendicular to the floor and the shin is parallel to the floor. Loop a rope around the bottom of your right foot and grasp the two ends of the rope with your right hand next to your right knee. Contract your quadriceps, thus straightening your right leg completely. Pull the rope toward your head until you feel a good stretch in your hamstrings. (You don't have to pull hard, just enough to feel that you're challenging the muscles.) Hold for 2 seconds, and relax by bending your right knee again. After completing 10 repetitions, stretch your left leg.

STRAIGHT-LEG HAMSTRINGS

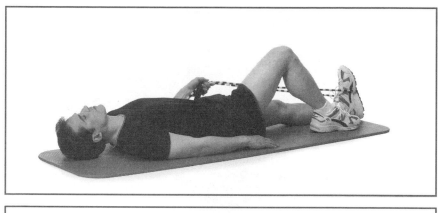

Loop a rope around the bottom of your left foot. Lie on your back with your left leg extended fully along the floor and your right leg bent slightly, with the foot resting flat on the floor. Hold the ends of the rope in your left hand at about the level of your upper thigh. By contracting your hip flexors, lift your left leg (keeping it completely straight) as high as you can. Extend this movement slightly with a gentle pull on the rope. Hold for 2 seconds, then relax. After completing 10 repetitions, stretch your right leg.

QUADRICEPS

Lie on your right side in a fetal position. Rest your head on the floor or on a pillow. Grasp the bottom of your right foot with your right hand and the top of your left foot with your left hand. By contracting the hamstrings and glutes, swing your left upper leg backward as far as possible. Extend this movement slightly by pulling with your left arm. Hold for 2 seconds, then relax. After completing 10 repetitions, stretch your right leg.

HIP FLEXORS

Stand on your right foot, bend your left leg fully, and hold your left foot in your hand behind you. By contracting your glutes and hamstrings, reach back as far as you can with your knee and bring your foot as close as you can to your lower back. Don't arch your back excessively while performing this stretch. Extend the movement slightly by pulling your foot toward your lower back with your hand. Hold for 2 seconds, then relax. After completing 10 repetitions, stretch your right leg.

GLUTES

Lie on your back with your left leg extended fully on the floor and your right leg bent 90 degrees and elevated so that the thigh is vertical. Place your left hand on your right hamstring just above the knee, and place your right hand on your right shin, just below the knee. By contracting your abdominal muscles and hip flexors, reach your right knee as far as possible toward your left shoulder. Use pressure from both hands to extend this movement slightly. Hold for 2 seconds at the end of the movement, then relax. After completing 10 repetitions, stretch your left side.

HIP ADDUCTORS

Lie on your back with both legs fully extended. Loop a rope around the bottom of your left foot. Wrap the two segments of the rope around your lower leg, and grasp them at the level of your upper thigh with your left hand. Grasp the ends in your right hand and rest them on your belly. Raise your left leg 1 inch above the floor. By contracting the muscles on the outside of your hip, sweep the left leg out to the side as far as you can. Extend this movement slightly by pulling the rope gently away from your body. Hold for 2 seconds, then relax. After completing 10 repetitions, stretch your right leg.

ACHILLES TENDON

Sit on the floor with your right leg outstretched in front of you and your left leg sharply bent so that the heel of the foot is as close to your butt as you can get it. With both hands, grasp the bottom of your left foot. Keeping your left heel in place, raise the toes of that foot off the floor and back toward your shin by contracting the muscles on the front of your shin. Use pressure from your hand to extend the motion slightly. Hold for 2 seconds, then relax. After completing 10 repetitions, stretch your right leg.

SOLEUS

Perform this stretch exactly as you would the Achilles tendon stretch on the opposite page, except bend the leg you're stretching to 90 degrees only instead of bending it fully.

GASTROCNEMIUS

Sit on the floor with both legs outstretched in front of you. Loop a rope around the bottom of your left forefoot. Hold the two segments of the rope in your hands with your arms outstretched, your torso upright, and tension in the rope. By contracting the muscles on the front of your shin, pull your toes as far as you can toward your body. Extend the motion slightly by pulling gently on the rope. Hold for 2 seconds, then relax. After completing 10 repetitions, stretch your right leg.

CONTRACT-RELAX STRETCHES

TRUNK ROTATORS

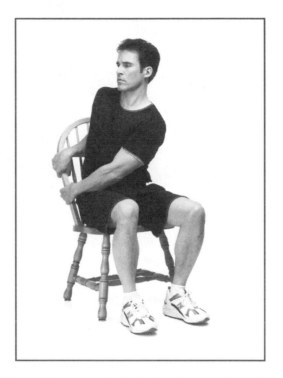

Sit comfortably upright in a straight-back chair. Twist to the right as far as comfortably possible, keeping your head aligned with your shoulders. When you reach the limit of your range of motion, grasp the side of the chair back with both hands to hold yourself in position. Now contract your back muscles as if to rotate back in the other direction, but use your arms to prevent any movement. Hold the contraction for 6 to 8 seconds, relax, then return to the starting position for one breath. Do 3 repetitions toward each side.

LOWER BACK

Sit upright in a chair with a folded towel stretched across your lower back, the ends of the towel held taut in your hands. Tip your torso forward by bending at the hips. Go as far as you comfortably can, making sure not to round your back. Now contract your lower-back muscles as if to raise yourself back upright, but prevent your torso from actually moving by pulling downward on both ends of the towel. Hold this contraction for 6 to 8 seconds and then relax for 2 or 3 seconds. Relax and return to the starting position for one breath. Shift the towel a few inches higher on your back, then repeat. Continue repeating until the towel reaches the level of your shoulder blades (four or five total stretches).

PIRIFORMIS

Lie faceup, bend your left leg to 90 degrees, and lift the left leg so that the thigh is perpendicular to the floor. Place your left hand on your left knee and your right hand on your lower left shin. Now rotate your left hip outward as you flex your hip abductors so that your lower leg swings inward and your entire left leg moves toward your head. Use very slight pressure from your hands to hold your leg in position at the end of this movement. You should feel a stretch deep in your left glute. Contract the same muscle you feel stretching, as if to reverse the movement you just completed, and use pressure from your hands to hold your leg in place. Hold the contraction for 6 to 8 seconds, relax, and return to the starting position for one breath. Repeat the stretch twice more, going farther each time. Then stretch your right side.

HIP FLEXORS

Stand in a split stance with your right foot positioned a large step ahead of your left, both feet flat on the floor, knees slightly bent, hands on hips. Rotate your pelvis backward and shift your weight forward and downward, bending your knees a bit more. You should feel a stretch at the front of your left hip. Contract this muscle as if you were going to take a forward step, but keep your weight on the leg so that it remains in place. Hold the contraction for 6 to 8 seconds, and then relax for one breath. Deepen the stretch twice more, then stretch your right side.

HIP ABDUCTORS

Lie faceup on the floor and bend your left leg sharply. Place your left foot flat on the floor next to your right knee and tip your left knee toward the floor to the right. You should feel a stretch on the outside of your hip. Contract this same muscle as if to swing your leg back in the opposite direction, but prevent it from doing so by placing your left hand on your left thigh and applying pressure. Hold the contraction for 6 to 8 seconds, relax, and return to the starting position for one breath. Deepen the stretch twice more, then stretch the right side.

HAMSTRINGS

Lie on your back with both legs extended fully. Loop a rope around the bottom of your left foot, and grasp both segments in your hands at about the level of your upper thigh. By contracting your left hip flexors, lift your left leg (keeping it completely straight) as high as you can. Pull the rope gently to hold your leg in place at the limit of your range of motion. Contract your left hamstrings as if to lower your leg again, but continue to hold it in place with the rope. Hold the contraction for 6 to 8 seconds, relax, and return to the starting position for one breath. Deepen the stretch by lifting your leg slightly higher twice more, then stretch your right leg.

QUADRICEPS

Lie facedown with your left leg bent fully. Reach behind your back with your right arm and grab your left foot. Stretch your left quadriceps by using your hand to gently pull the foot slightly closer to your buttocks. Contract your quadriceps as if to straighten your leg again, but prevent it from moving with resistance from your hand. Hold the contraction for 6 to 8 seconds, relax, and return to the starting position for one breath. Deepen the stretch by bending your leg a bit more two more times, then stretch your right leg.

GASTROCNEMIUS AND SOLEUS

Stretch the gastrocnemius first. Sit upright on the floor with both legs extended straight in front of you. Loop a rope around the bottom of your left foot, and grasp the two segments in your hands at about the level of your knees. Contract the muscles on the front of your left shin, and try to pull your toes toward your knee as far as possible. Pull gently on the rope to assist the stretch. Contract your left calf as if to point your toes, but hold your foot in place by pulling harder on the rope. Hold the contraction for 6 to 8 seconds, relax for one breath, then deepen the stretch by bringing your toes closer to your knee twice more.

Bend your left knee to 90 degrees and repeat this stretch, using your hands to provide resistance instead of the rope. Bending the knee moves the stretch from the gastrocnemius to the soleus. Then stretch the opposite leg.

YOGA STRETCHES

I recommend performing these six yoga poses in a sequence wherein you move smoothly and without interruption from one to the next. The poses are ordered to make this easy to do. Try to complete the full sequence two or three times.

FORWARD BEND

(HAMSTRINGS, BUTTOCKS, LOWER BACK)

Stand comfortably and bend forward at the pelvis and waist, reaching toward the floor with both hands. Go as far as you can without discomfort. Pause, exhale, and then place your palms flat on the floor in front of your feet. (You'll probably have to bend your knees slightly to accomplish this.) Inhale and straighten your legs again. Exhale and return your palms to the floor.

DOWN DOG

(CALVES, HAMSTRINGS)

From the forward bend position, walk your hands forward so that your body forms an inverted V. Go no farther than you can without your heels coming off the floor. Hold for 30 seconds while breathing slowly, pressing your heels into the floor, and trying to relax every muscle in your body as much as possible.

COBRA

(HIP FLEXORS, ABDOMEN)

From the down dog position, swoop headfirst downward, forward, and back up again as though you were trying to sneak underneath a low barbed wire. You will end up in an arched pushup position. Hold for 20 seconds while breathing slowly and trying to relax your whole body.

LUNGE

(HIP FLEXORS, HAMSTRINGS, HIP ADDUCTORS, CALVES)

From the cobra position, draw your right leg forward and place the foot next to and just outside your right hand. Lower your elbows to the floor and lace your fingers together. Bend the knee of your right leg as much as necessary to achieve this position, but no more. (It's okay for your right heel to come off the floor.) Hold for 20 seconds while breathing slowly and trying to relax your whole body. Reverse the position, extending the right leg backward and drawing the left forward. Hold for 20 seconds.

SPINE TWIST

(LOWER BACK, OBLIQUES, HAMSTRINGS, CALVES)

From the lunge position, raise your torso slightly and plant your right fist on the floor just inside your right foot. Straighten this arm completely and use it to support a share of your weight. Twist your torso to the left and raise your left arm straight overhead. Turn your head in the same direction so that you can see your upraised hand. Hold for 20 seconds while breathing slowly and trying to relax your whole body. Reverse your position, twist to the other side, and hold again for 20 seconds.

BOW POSE

(HIP FLEXORS, QUADRICEPS, ABDOMEN, CHEST, SHOULDERS)

From the spine twist position, lie facedown on the floor. Bend both legs, reach behind your body with both arms, and grasp the tops of your feet. Pull upward so that your head, torso, and thighs come off the ground as far as possible. Look forward and slightly upward. Hold for 20 seconds while breathing slowly and eliminating all unnecessary muscle tension.

STRETCHLIKE THERAPEUTIC EXERCISES

Lengthening the muscles through movement and positioning of the limbs is the most effective way to increase functional range of motion. But there is another, rather different way to increase mobility in various parts of the body that can serve as a supplement to the forms of stretching I've just demonstrated. The idea is to lengthen the muscles in the same way you flatten bread dough with a rolling pin, but instead of a rolling pin (ouch!) you use a therapeutic foam roller like the one pictured. (They are available from many physical-therapy offices and exercise-equipment retailers.)

Three parts of the body in particular benefit from these foam-roller exercises: the spine, the buttocks, and the iliotibial band.

SPINE MOBILIZATION EXERCISE

This exercise helps to increase spine mobility and correct posture. Sit on the floor with your knees bent and feet flat on the floor. Place a foam roller on the floor behind you, positioned so that it will run across your back just beneath the shoulder blades when you lie back. Support your neck in your hands with your fingers laced together and elbows wide. Slowly lean backward until your spine comes into contact with the foam roller. Even more slowly, ease your weight onto the roller. You should feel the vertebra in this area "releasing," which may be slightly uncomfortable at first but should not be painful. Go back as far as you can comfortably go, and hold for 3 to 5 seconds.

After returning to the start position, move the foam roller 2 inches closer to your butt and repeat. Move the roller twice more to mobilize all the vertebrae in the thoracic (midback) section of your spine.

ILIOTIBIAL BAND MASSAGE

This exercise uses the "rolling pin principle" to lengthen the iliotibial band. I once used it to put a quick end to a nagging case of iliotibial band syndrome, wherein the IT band becomes tight and begins to rub during running, causing pain and inflammation. It works fast, but it can be quite painful. Lie on your side with a foam roller positioned crossways beneath your upper thigh. Keep your legs straight and both feet off the floor. Use your arms to slowly drag yourself forward while causing the roller to roll so that it squeezes your IT band from just below the hip to just above the knee. Walk your hands in the opposite direction for a reverse squeeze. Do this a few times, then repeat on the other side. It gets less painful when you do it consistently.

BUTTOCK TRIGGER-POINT RELEASE

A trigger point is an area of concentrated tightness and tenderness that develops in a muscle. The piriformis, located deep inside the buttock, is a classic trigger point in runners. Releasing it through the therapeutic application of pressure can increase the mobility of your hips and reduce pain or tenderness in this area.

Sit on a foam roller, place your left ankle on your right thigh, and shift most of your weight onto your left buttock. Roll very slowly backward and forward on the roller until you find the point of maximum tenderness. Get as much pressure as you can on this precise spot, and try to let your muscles relax (the gluteal muscles naturally contract to protect the piriformis from the pressure). You will suddenly feel your gluteal muscles release, and you will actually sink down into the roller another quarter-inch or so. The tenderness will increase as the roller gets more direct access to your piriformis. Continue for about 20 seconds, and then release the other side.

FOUR

ENDURANCE CROSS-TRAINING

I USE THE TERM *endurance cross-training* when I'm talking about non-impact forms of cardiovascular exercise such as pool running and bicycling. There are a few different ways that runners can incorporate those and other types of endurance cross-training into their programs. What's best for you depends on your needs, goals, experience, and preferences—just as with any other kind of training.

I believe that endurance cross-training has at least seven distinct purposes.

1. You can use it to prevent injuries by reducing impact and/or correcting muscular imbalances.

2. It helps you maintain fitness while rehabilitating injuries that restrict your running.

3. You can improve your running fitness by increasing your strength, power, and/or economy via activities chosen specifically for such purposes.

4. You can use it for active recovery from a race or a hard workout.

5. It helps you maintain or even enhance your motivation by adding variety to your training experience.

6. You can dabble in other endurance sports—such as triathlon or adventure racing—and still maintain your running-specific fitness.

7. In the off-season, you can cross-train your way to a rejuvenated body and mind.

From that group of benefits and a universe of possible ways to achieve them, I think we can identify three general approaches to endurance cross-training that together encompass the needs of all runners.

First is the **MINIMALIST** approach. This is for those who have little interest in endurance activities other than running or who are completely focused on racing and have no special physical needs that require them to do more than the minimum amount of cross-training. My recommendation for these runners is that they typically perform one endurance cross-training workout per week for active recovery. When injured or especially sore, they can replace individual runs with endurance cross-training workouts as necessary.

Second is the **SPECIAL NEEDS** approach for runners who are especially injury-prone or have other weaknesses that the minimalist approach can't help. These runners may find themselves doing an endurance cross-training workout for every run. If you fall into this category, you'll most likely try a variety of activities and ratios before you figure out what works best. Take, for example, a very lithe runner who has two problems: recurring shin splints and lack of muscular strength. For her, the perfect weekly cross-training schedule might include three or four running workouts and two or three bicycle rides. Cycling deals with both of her problems: It builds leg strength and lets her avoid the repetitive impact that causes shin splints in the first place.

Finally, there's the **MAXIMALIST** approach, which satisfies the needs of runners who simply enjoy participating in other endurance activities and may also compete in other endurance sports. The runners in this group can do more or less whatever they please—that's the point— as long as they avoid three possible problems.

1. Doing more total training than they can handle

2. Running so little that their running performance slips

3. Training inappropriately for their alternative endurance sport or sports (overtraining, undertraining, creating muscular imbalances, et cetera)

HOW TO CHOOSE?

The choice of the perfect endurance cross-training system isn't always obvious. Sure, if you're a serious runner and casual triathlete, it's pretty straightforward—you add swimming and cycling to your schedule. But what if you're a cross-training minimalist who's never done anything besides run? You want to do active-recovery workouts in an appropriate discipline that won't bore you to death, but you may have no idea where to begin.

The rest of this chapter provides the information you need to choose the best activities and use them effectively. This is by no means a complete list—not one word about skipping rope!—but I think the six endurance activities I describe are the most beneficial, practical, and interesting for runners. I list them in the order I'd recommend them to a cross-training minimalist who's primarily interested in using them for active recovery.

I go into the most detail on bicycling and swimming because triathlon, in my experience, is a sport many runners are interested in pursuing.

POOL RUNNING

ADVANTAGES: Also called deep-water running, this is the most running-specific form of endurance cross-training, involving more or less the same action as land running but with greater resistance and virtually no impact. That puts it at the top of the list for injured runners. Runners who've used pool running for extended periods of rehabilitation when unable to run on land tell me that making the adjustment back to land running is surprisingly easy. You do lose some timing, which returns quickly, and you do have to readjust to the impact involved in conventional running. But you don't lose fitness. And pool running can be performed by runners with a wider variety of injuries than any other activity except swimming.

Even when you aren't injured, pool running is ideal for active-recovery workouts. It's unlikely to hinder muscle-tissue repair, and it might even accelerate muscle recovery—all this while actually increasing your running-specific fitness because water provides a form of resistance that strengthens your running stride. You'd probably run better after a month of pool running than after a month of bicycling or inline skating. In fact, in 1982, Mary Decker broke the 2000m world

SUMMARY OF ENDURANCE CROSS-TRAINING MODALITIES

MODALITY	ADVANTAGES	DISADVANTAGES
Pool Running	Highly running-specific Totally non-weight-bearing Minimal muscle tissue stress	Boring to some Requires pool access Lessens shock-absorption capacity of legs
Elliptical Training	Running-specific Builds strength Can increase stride rate	Requires elliptical trainer Boring to some
Bicycling	Complements muscular development of running Builds leg strength Can increase stride rate	Less running-specific
Inline Skating	Complements muscular development of running Builds leg strength	Requires smooth surface
Swimming	Essential for triathlons Spares the legs	Not running-specific Requires pool access Very technique-intensive
Cross-Country Skiing	More intense than running Fun	Requires snow

record after running in a pool for several weeks while rehabilitating a stress fracture.

DISADVANTAGES: Pool running isn't the absolute best endurance cross-training choice for every runner. For those runners who may need to substantially increase leg strength or improve muscle balance, bicycling may be a better option. And injured runners facing a long rehabilitation may lose some lower-body bone density if they train exclusively in the pool, since bones grow stronger with high-impact activities and weaker without it. A loss of bone mass means your body has less natural shock absorption, and that could lead to stress fractures or other impact-related injuries when you return to dry land. So if you're faced with a long rehabilitation, it's best to mix in a weight-bearing form of endurance cross-training, such as elliptical training, and return to full-impact running slowly and carefully—initially running only on sand and grass, for example.

Perhaps the greatest drawback of pool running is that it is, in the opinion of most runners who've done it, rather boring. This is less of an issue when you're doing only 30-minute active-recovery workouts than when you're injured and trying to simulate interval workouts and long runs in the pool.

Another restriction of pool running is, of course, the pool. Unless you happen to live a block from the YMCA or in a house or apartment complex with a heated or indoor lap pool, pool running will probably be less convenient (and perhaps more expensive) than some other forms of cross-training.

EQUIPMENT: Besides a pool, you'll also need a flotation belt made specifically for water running. The belt allows you to float immersed at shoulder level and to maintain a proper, upright posture while running. Without a belt, you'll have to devote more energy to keeping your head above water than to moving forward, and you'll end up running in a crouched position. Thus, wearing the belt results in a workout that better simulates land running.

The most popular brand is the Aqua Jogger. Many larger running specialty stores carry pool-running belts, and you can also buy them online. Expect to pay about $45.

TECHNIQUE: The first time you try pool running, concentrate on your form rather than on the intensity or duration of your workout. Most athletes will have a natural tendency to perform an action that's more like treading water than running. Your goal is to emulate your land-running stride as closely as possible or to use a slightly idealized version of that form. In other words, use a stride that looks more like sprinting than like jogging.

The most common error is running in place instead of moving forward. You'll automatically improve your form when you try to make forward progress. Concentrate on not just lifting your thighs but also reaching out with the forward foot, pushing off, and extending the push-off leg fully behind you. Couple this action with a strong but more or less natural arm swing. (Your shoulders may quickly become fatigued in your first few pool runs because of the greater resistance of the liquid medium.) Other common form flaws to avoid are hunching the shoulders and leaning forward at the waist.

Workouts: When doing recovery workouts, simply immerse yourself in water that is deeper than shoulder height, and run either in circles or back and forth for 20 to 60 minutes, starting slowly and then maintaining a steady low-to-moderate level of effort. When you're injured, perform pool workouts that imitate as closely as possible the duration, intensity, and structure of the land-running workouts you would be performing if you were healthy. For example, if you were scheduled to perform a dozen quarter-mile repeats on the track at 90 seconds per quarter, perform 12 hard 90-second intervals in the pool, separated by rest intervals that also match what you normally do on the track. Be sure to warm up and cool down as you normally would.

Intensity is the tricky part. In the pool, you can't use pace to gauge intensity, and it's equally hard to go by feel. Most elite runners use heart rate monitors or take manual pulse readings when doing pool workouts. Of course, you first have to know what your heart rate is at various intensities on land. In the example given above, you would need to know what your heart rate tends to be at the end of a quarter-mile interval. Then you'd need to subtract 10 to 15 beats from that number, since it's impossible to get your heart rate as high in the pool as on land. So if your heart rate is typically about 177 at the end of a quarter-mile interval, it should be around 162 to 167 at the end of your 90-second interval in the pool.

In general, expect to have to run more intensively in the water to achieve a workout that's equivalent to what you would achieve on land. In studies involving untrained subjects, those who ran on land got in shape much faster than those who did an equivalent amount of running in the pool, because the latter subjects did not train as intensely, on average. These results don't mean you can't get a great running workout in the pool; they just mean you have to concentrate on it.

ELLIPTICAL TRAINING

Equipment/advantages: The elliptical trainer was invented in the 1990s by Precor, a fitness-equipment maker already well-known for its treadmills. The idea was to simulate the action of running without the impact—something the machines did so successfully that they quickly became standard equipment in gyms. Now manufactured by a number of companies, elliptical trainers may also be purchased for home use, but they're quite expensive. An entry-level machine will set you back at least $1,000; a club-quality machine will cost $2,500 or more.

An elliptical trainer looks somewhat similar to a stairclimbing machine, and its action feels like a mix of stairclimbing and cross-country skiing. The only cardiovascular activity that's more similar to running is pool running. The key difference: While elliptical training involves no impact, it is a weight-bearing activity. Thus, pool running is a better choice for runners who have injuries that make it impossible or inadvisable to perform any weight-bearing exercise, but elliptical training is better for helping you maintain your body's impact-absorbing capacity.

Because the elliptical-training action is not exactly like running, it's a good way to round out your running fitness. Specifically, by recruiting and conditioning muscle fibers that running misses, it can strengthen your legs, your core muscles, and the muscles involved in the arm swing.

Some machines come with arm levers; some don't. If you want to use elliptical training for increased core and upper-body strength, you need to use one with levers.

DISADVANTAGES: On the psychological level, many runners find elliptical training to be slightly less tedious than pool running—you can listen to music or watch television while doing it. Still, there's no getting around the fact that for most runners, elliptical training is pretty darned boring.

WORKOUTS: Recovery workouts should entail 20 to 60 minutes of movement at a low-to-moderate level of intensity. When you're injured, perform elliptical workouts that as closely as possible match the duration, intensity, and structure of the land-running workouts you would be performing if healthy. For example, if your training schedule calls for a 20-minute threshold run on a given day, do 20 minutes of elliptical training at a comfortably hard intensity level, preceded by an easy warmup and followed by an easy cooldown.

The best way to control intensity on an elliptical trainer is to monitor your heart rate. Many machines have built-in pulse monitors, but you can always use your own monitor if you have one. (Yours is probably more accurate.)

If you're interested in using elliptical training to round out your running fitness, I suggest you perform two weekly recovery workouts on the machine rather than just one. You need to stimulate those muscle-recruitment patterns at least every 3 days in order to accumulate gains in neuromuscular efficiency and muscle-fiber conditioning. Most elliptical trainers allow you to vary resistance, and some allow you to adjust the incline to simulate hills. Increasing either the resistance or the incline increases the strength-building effect. Just be sure that you stay within your desired intensity range.

I believe that elliptical trainers also have the potential to increase your natural stride rate. By keeping the resistance (and incline) low, you can fairly easily maintain a stride rate as high as 180 strides per minute, the cadence most elite runners use. Over time, your neuromotor system will gain efficiency at this stride rate, and in theory you should get some transfer back to running.

BICYCLING

ADVANTAGES: Back in the day, bicycling (outdoors and indoors) was more or less the only form of endurance cross-training runners used. It was, for example, Frank Shorter's cross-training activity of choice. In recent years, alternatives like pool running and elliptical training have eroded its monopoly, but cycling remains popular among runners. As a repetitive-motion activity in which the legs do the work, it develops a form of fitness that's highly transferable to running. Many elite road cyclists can run an excellent 10-K on the basis of their bike training alone. But unlike running, cycling is a nonimpact activity, so it can serve runners well as a recovery or rehabilitation workout. The same guidelines that apply to other endurance cross-training modalities apply to cycling.

DISADVANTAGES: The main disadvantage of outdoor cycling, besides the cost of buying a bike, is that in many climates it's difficult if not impossible to train year-round. An important limitation of indoor cycling is that it requires no balance and therefore does not emulate this neuromuscular aspect of running as well as outdoor cycling and other endurance cross-training options do.

EQUIPMENT: In order to do any amount of riding, you need a bike, of course. The best kind for you depends on how you want to use it. If you want a bike that is light enough and has enough gears to get you up and over hills but you also want some comfort and don't plan to race, your best choice will be a comfort bike or a hybrid. If you plan to do some rough off-road riding, you'll need a mountain bike. (Comfort bikes and hybrids can handle light off-road use.) If you intend to ride exclusively on pavement and you want something fast, use either a road or time-trial bike. The latter is designed to be ridden in the so-called aero position, in which your torso is nearly parallel to the ground and your forearms rest close together on a time-trial handlebar. As its name suggests, this position is extremely aerodynamic, making time-trial bikes the fastest bikes on flat terrain. However, standard road bikes are more versatile, and you can achieve a pretty good aero position on a road bike by installing a clip-on aerobar and moving the seat forward slightly. This is the better way to go for most runner-cyclists and runner-triathletes.

Comfort and hybrid bikes are generally the least expensive; you can get a new one from a reputable manufacturer for about $350. Mountain bikes are a little more expensive, starting in the $600 range. Road bikes are more expensive still ($1,000 at entry level), while time-trial bikes (also called triathlon bikes) are the most expensive at $1,200 and up.

If you plan to do hard training (and possibly even some racing) on a road, mountain, or time-trial bike, it's essential that you get the fit right, and unless you know a lot about bikes, you'll need some professional help. (If you're buying a bike for just cruising around, you can afford to be less fanatical about fit.) The best bike shops have honest, knowledgeable salespeople who make a genuine effort to match you with the best bike for your needs. These shops are in the minority, so be sure to do a little research before you decide where to buy. You could very easily purchase an ill-fitting or poorly adjusted bike if your salesperson isn't well-trained or just doesn't care.

A helmet is mandatory for outdoor cycling. Sports sunglasses are virtually a must-have as well. If you ride a high-performance road bike with a lightweight seat, you'll almost certainly want to wear padded bike shorts to make the riding experience infinitely more comfortable. And if you're at all serious about your riding, it's best to use cycling shoes that clip on to the pedals and allow you to generate force more evenly throughout the pedal stroke. A basic pair of cycling shoes and set of clip-on pedals will cost you about $200.

I strongly recommend that you learn how to use a tire repair kit ($10 to $15) and carry one on every ride—you never know when you'll need to fix or replace a punctured inner tube. (Almost any bike-shop mechanic will gladly show you how to fix a flat.) One last, extremely handy item is a bike computer that records distance traveled, speed, and so forth. You can get a basic one for less than $50.

BILL RODGERS

Believe it or not, the original "modern" distance runners of the late 19th and early 20th centuries trained primarily by walking. It worked pretty well, because walking is more like running than it may seem to those of us who tend to disdain it. It's hard to achieve the same level of intensity in walking as in running, so I don't recommend walking as a substitute for high-intensity workouts during periods of injury rehabilitation. However, I do highly recommend that runners perform some walking during extended layoffs from running (when possible). It's a low-impact rather than a nonimpact modality, so it keeps the bones and joints of the lower extremities in a better state of readiness for the pounding of running than, say, elliptical training does.

This is precisely how the great Bill Rodgers used walking while rehabilitating, at age 55, from a stress fracture, his first major injury in 38 years of running. Indeed, Rodgers's resiliency is a big part of what made him the most accomplished American marathoner of all time. In the 1970s and 1980s, he won the New York City Marathon and the Boston Marathon each four times. He ran 2 marathons under 2:10, 4 under 2:11, and 28 under 2:15. And he once won 7 marathons in a row.

But his aura of invincibility crumbled when his right tibia suddenly snapped as he was completing a routine 8-miler. He was forced to spend 3 months in a rigid cast and 3 weeks in a walking cast. As soon as he could begin walking again, he did. He proceeded cautiously but aggressively, increasing the duration of his walks as quickly as safety allowed. He also rode a stationary bike to drive his cardiorespiratory system back into shape. When he was able to begin running again, he followed the same gentle but steady progression.

He suffered his injury in August 2003. In February 2004, he completed his first comeback race, a 5-K. You can't keep "Boston Billy" down for long!

From a physiological perspective, it doesn't matter whether you ride outdoors or in. The main advantage of riding outdoors is that in the right environment, it's a total blast. For those who don't own an indoor cycle machine, a bike is also more convenient because you can zoom right out your garage door instead of having to drive to the nearest fitness club. On the other hand, indoor riding is safer (no cars, dogs, or hairpin turns), and some find it more comfortable. You can wear whatever you want, since you're always at room temperature, and you don't have to worry about wind, rain, sleet, or snow.

If you own a road, mountain, or time-trial bike, you can convert it to indoor use by mounting it on rollers or a fluid trainer, available for $90 and up at most shops that sell racing bikes. This gives you the option of riding outside or in. A more expensive alternative is to buy a club-style indoor cycling machine. The decent ones begin at $900.

TECHNIQUE: To ride safely and proficiently, you'll need to learn a few important skills: positioning (there are several hand positions you can use on a road bike), pedaling mechanics, gear selection, braking, cornering, climbing, and descending.

The more miles you put on the bike, the better you'll develop these skills. However, you can accelerate the learning process by riding with a more experienced cyclist, taking lessons from a coach, or reading cycling magazines and books and visiting specialized Web sites (such as www.bicycling.com).

WORKOUTS: Recovery workouts on the bike should entail 20 to 60 minutes at a steady low-to-moderate level of intensity. When you're injured, perform bike workouts that as closely as possible match the duration, intensity, and structure of the running workouts you would be performing if healthy.

Bob Kennedy, America's great 5000-meter runner, used the bike in this way. When he was injured, he'd perform sets of 2-minute bursts on his bike instead of 800-meter repeats on the track. If you choose to use a heart rate monitor to control intensity on the bike, be aware that at any given effort level, your heart rate will be about 10 beats per minute slower than during running.

There is a possible exception to the matching-workouts rule. Because cycling is impact-free and less intense than running, you may decide to go out on rides that are significantly longer than any run workout you'd ever perform. Rides of 3 to 5 hours will enhance your general endurance without taking any more out of you than a 2-hour run.

As a triathlete, I've found that my long rides provide a tremendous boost to my running endurance. Note that long-term rehabilitative cycling is likely to result in less degradation of the legs' shock-absorption capacity than pool running, but more than elliptical training.

I'm sure you've noticed that cyclists tend to have more muscular legs than runners have. This is because cycling uses less total muscle mass to overcome greater average resistance. Muscles that are made to work harder tend to grow more. Cycling, therefore, is a terrific way for runners to develop better leg strength and power.

There's also a neuromotor benefit of cross-training on the bike. In a University of Colorado study, on three separate occasions a group of triathletes completed a 30-minute bike workout followed by a 2-mile maximum-effort run. In the first trial, the triathletes pedaled at normal cadence. In the second, they pedaled 20 percent faster than normal, and in the third, 20 percent slower than normal. As a group, the subjects ran the fastest times and had higher stride rates following high-cadence cycling.

At race intensity, elite runners take about 180 strides (90 steps per foot) per minute; nearly all other runners take fewer strides. On the bike, it's easy to pedal 90 revolutions per minute as long as you ride on flat or downhill terrain and use an appropriate gear (or resistance level if you're on a stationary bike). I believe runners can accomplish over the long term what the triathletes in the experiment did in the short term; that is, through a neuromotor crossover effect, you can increase your efficiency at higher stride rates and become a faster runner.

A runner who's interested in using cycling to increase his or her strength, power, and efficiency should ride at least twice a week most weeks. Cross-training minimalists should perform at least one bike-recovery workout per week (assuming that cycling is their endurance cross-training activity of choice), plus additional workouts when they are especially sore or feel that they're on the verge of an overuse injury.

DUATHLON/TRIATHLON: Many runners get the urge to try a multi-sport race. This can be a fairly easy transition as long as you don't make the mistake I made the first time I tried it. I jumped into an Olympic-distance triathlon (1.5-K swim, 40-K bike, 10-K run) on a lark, confident that my run training would carry me through. Never in my life have I suffered more in a race, nor finished so close to dead last. Needless to say, I balanced my training in all three disciplines before my next triathlon.

The principles and methods of bike training are quite similar to those of running, so it's easy to get into the swing of it (though gaining strength on the bike takes time). When you're training for a triathlon or duathlon, most of your rides should be performed at a steady moderate intensity. Once a week or so, you should do a long ride that tests your cycling endurance. And a small amount of your training should be at higher intensities in an interval format, just as you'd do for running. (In chapter 7, I'll present a detailed training program for runners preparing for a first triathlon.)

INLINE SKATING

ADVANTAGES: Inline skating, like running, is all about the legs. But the lower-body muscles that do the most work during inline skating are those that do the least while running. Inline skating works mainly the buttocks, hip abductors (outer hip muscles), quadriceps, and shins; running, as we've discussed, focuses on the gluteals, hamstrings, and calves.

The fact that inline skating is a kind of muscular mirror image of running makes it a great cross-training choice for a runner who's interested in rounding out the muscular development of the lower body and in preventing or correcting the muscular imbalances that so often contribute to overuse injuries. Inline skating entails greater average resistance than running, so it's also a good overall leg strengthener.

The other great thing about inline skating is that it's fun. It has many of the same virtues as running, yet it's faster, and there's something ineffably satisfying about the feeling of gliding.

DISADVANTAGES: The main disadvantage of skating is that it's no fun at all unless you're on a very smooth surface, so you're much more limited in terms of where you can go on skates than you are on foot. Inclement weather is also more likely to foil skating than running. However, you can get around this problem by purchasing a slide board that allows you to skate in place, in your stocking feet, indoors.

EQUIPMENT: Skating requires skates, of course. There are many varieties; you want the kind called fitness skates. Racing skates, featuring a longer wheelbase with five wheels instead of four, are best avoided by beginner and even intermediate skaters. Expect to pay between $110 and $170 for a high-quality pair of new fitness skates. The best place to buy them is at a specialty store from a salesperson who skates, rather than at one of those sporting-goods mega-stores. Tell the salesperson where and how you intend to use the skates, ask for recommendations, and try on at least three models. The fit should be quite snug but not constricting.

Wheel types and sizes vary even more than the skates themselves. Larger and harder wheels tend to be faster, while smaller and softer wheels tend to offer more control. Wheels wear more quickly on the outside edge, so you'll need to rotate them when they begin to look worn on that side and replace them once they're worn on both sides. (This is very easy.) Buy a helmet (about $40) at the same time you buy your skates, and wear it for every skating workout. Hand pads are recommended for all skaters as well, and beginners will also want to wear knee and elbow pads. Complete pad sets can be purchased for $40 or so.

TECHNIQUE: If you are a beginner, before you begin doing actual workouts on inline skates, you need to devote a couple of sessions to practicing three basic skills: striding, stopping, and falling. The stride comes quickly. Find a flat, smooth surface and begin by getting your stance right: Bend your knees a little and shift most of your weight onto your heels. If you can't lift your toes to the top of the boot, your center of gravity is too far forward. Form a V with your skates and begin walking forward, maintaining the V. Use your arms for balance.

Once you get comfortable walking in skates, try to glide a bit. Begin with both skates in full contact with the ground, in the V shape, and push off with the left skate to make the right skate glide diagonally forward. Touch down with the left skate and then push off with the right to glide on the left. Keep trying to glide farther and farther, seeing how far you can go on one skate. Once you're able to glide with steady balance, try skating with one hand grasping the opposite wrist behind your back, as doing so is more energy efficient than anything else you might do with your arms.

There are various braking systems on inline skates, but they're all more or less versions of a rubber pad and plastic arm attached to the heel of your skate. (On most good models, the brake arm may be attached to either skate; put it on your dominant side.) To use the brake, position your feet side by side, slide the braking skate forward, and then dip your heel toward the ground until the rubber pad makes contact and begins to drag. This asymmetrical drag and deceleration will challenge your balance at first, so start slowly. Some beginners find it helpful to practice balancing on one skate before they practice braking. There are fancier ways to brake, such as V stops and hockey stops, but you should master the basic technique before you try any others.

Falling is all but inevitable for beginners. Unless you practice correct falling technique, you will experience more pain than necessary. Falling backward is the worst-case scenario, because you'll almost certainly hit rear end first and really jar your tailbone. From there, you could very well fall back and whack your head. So when you begin to fall backward, twist around to one side as you go, and try to absorb the impact on the knee and elbow pads on that side. Splitting the impact 50/50 in this manner will greatly reduce your chance of injury. Find a grassy spot and practice turning a backward fall into a side fall.

If you fall forward, don't throw your arms out to take the impact on your hands, as most skaters instinctively do. Instead, throw your knees down and land first on your kneepads, *then* throw your arms out and *slide* forward on your hands and knees, keeping your torso off the pavement.

A final note: Due to the slightly forward leaning posture it requires, skating places stress on the lower back that can lead to muscle strains. To avoid these injuries, be sure to consistently perform strengthening exercises for all of the core muscles (lower back, obliques, and abdominals).

WORKOUTS: The appropriate format for active-recovery workouts involving inline skating is 20 to 60 minutes at a steady low-to-moderate level of intensity. Granted, Olympian Steve Plasencia used to perform 90-minute high-intensity "active-recovery" workouts on skates. Far be it from me to call him crazy. The fact is that all of the endurance cross-training guidelines I offer are just guidelines. Of course it's possible for runners to benefit from long- and/or high-intensity endurance cross-training, but in general, I do think it's best to keep these workouts relatively short and easy. At least start there to see how it goes.

One weekly active-recovery skate is enough for most runners, but you may do more if you wish. In cases of injury, perform skate workouts that are similar in format to the run workouts you would be doing if you were healthy. If you use a heart rate monitor to control intensity, note that your heart rate will be roughly 10 beats per minute slower at any given effort level on skates than on foot.

SWIMMING

ADVANTAGES: In swimming, the arms produce far more force than the legs. For this reason, swimming has less crossover fitness benefit for runners than do the other endurance activities discussed in this chapter, all of which are more similar to running in their reliance on the legs.

Because swimming does give the cardiovascular, metabolic, and endocrine systems a proper workout without stressing the tissues of the legs, it is a perfectly good way for runners to get an active-recovery or rehabilitative workout. I recommend swimming to runners who enjoy it more than other endurance cross-training activities, who have serious injuries that make it inadvisable or impossible to perform leg-reliant activities, or who would like to try a triathlon. Other runners would do best to choose a different activity for endurance cross-training workouts.

DISADVANTAGES: In situations of prolonged rehabilitation, swimming has the same disadvantage as pool running in that it is completely non-weight-bearing and therefore results in steady degradation of the lower extremities' shock-absorption capacity.

The other great disadvantage of swimming, for those who lack extensive swimming experience, is that it is an extremely technique-intensive sport. Mastering freestyle swimming technique is not easy. There are three strategies you can use to progress along the technique learning curve as rapidly as possible. The most effective strategy is to have another person watch, critique, and correct your stroke. The person could be an experienced swimmer who uses the same facility you use, a coach with a masters swim program, a private coach, or someone else who knows the difference between correct and incorrect freestyle technique. Watching others swim is a nice complement to having others watch you. I own an instructional swim video that features lots of underwater footage of good swimmers. I watch it frequently and feel it has helped me quite a bit.

Another effective strategy is to regularly perform drills designed to improve technique in various elements of the freestyle stroke. A third way to develop your swim technique is, instead of doing slower, uninterrupted swims, to perform relatively short, fast intervals in which you really concentrate on form. Technique tends to improve with speed, while taking frequent breaks prevents the fatigue that tends to impair form.

TECHNIQUE: There are five components of the freestyle swim stroke: body position, body roll, arm stroke, kick, and breathing. The most important components of the stroke, it may surprise you to hear, are the first two. This is because, in swimming, eliminating drag does a lot more to increase speed than generating force does, and proper body positioning and good body roll are the most effective ways to eliminate drag. When you are positioned correctly, your chest is the most deeply submerged part of your body, your head is tilted just slightly forward, and your legs are floating high in the water. This position maximizes buoyancy and thereby minimizes drag. With each stroke, as your leading arm achieves full forward extension, you need to rotate your entire body as much as 60 degrees toward the opposite side in order to achieve a narrow, torpedo-like profile.

Perform the arm cycle as follows. Put your hand in the water 12 to 18 inches in front of your shoulder. Reach as far forward as possible, with your hand about a foot or so beneath the surface, and rotate your body to the opposite side the way you do when trying to grab something off a high shelf. Thrust your shoulder forward, toward your ear, while rotating your hand and forearm 90 degrees so that your fingers point straight toward the bottom of the pool. You should feel water resistance against your entire forearm and hand. Next, with an accelerating movement, draw your hand straight underneath your body, keeping your elbow high and bent 90 degrees until your hand passes your ribcage, at which point you extend your arm and continue pushing until your hand exits the water right next to your upper thigh. Lastly, carry your arm forward to prepare for the next hand entry. Keep your elbow high, and let your forearm and hand dangle toward the water. Your arms should always be at opposite points in the arm cycle. When one arm is just reaching full extension in front of you, the other hand should be just exiting the water at your upper thigh, and so forth.

The kick serves a minor role in propulsion (except during sprints and brief surges) and a greater role in maintaining stroke rhythm and proper body position. The form of kicking used in freestyle swimming is called the flutter kick. It is a small, up-and-down scissor motion in which the two legs are always moving in opposite directions, as the arms are in running. A good kick is small in amplitude, very steady, and initiated from the hips and buttocks rather than at the knee. Keep your toes pointed, and flex the knee only slightly at the top of the kick. The proper rhythm for flutter kicking is two kicks per foot per arm stroke.

It is important that you do not allow your stroke to interfere with your breathing, nor your breathing to interfere with your stroke. Exhale via forceful blowing through the mouth, underwater, as you stroke. When exhalation is complete, inhale by turning your head just slightly at the top of your body rotation and sucking in all the air you can get during the brief moment when your face comes out of the water. This extra movement of the head should be as subtle as possible.

Less experienced swimmers tend to always breathe on the same side every two or four strokes. Better swimmers practice bilateral breathing, constantly alternating the side on which they inhale, every three to five strokes. The main advantage of being able to breathe on both sides is that it promotes symmetrical swim mechanics. You should definitely make it a point to learn bilateral breathing by practicing it for a few lengths at a time until it becomes second nature.

I will talk about workouts for performance in swimming in chapter 7, where I present a triathlon training program for runners. Here, I wish only to describe a set of drills you should perform each time you swim, until you've really mastered the freestyle stroke. Do a few lengths (a length is one trip across the pool, usually 25 yards or meters) of each drill in the order presented, resting as often as necessary between lengths.

- **Chest press.** Swim with your arms at your sides and propel yourself by kicking only. Exhale into the water and turn your head to the side to inhale. Concentrate on keeping your chest deep and your hips and legs high, toward the surface. This drill improves body position and kicking technique.

- **Side kicking.** Swim on one side with your lower arm extended straight forward and your upper arm resting on your upper side. Rest your head against your shoulder and look down so that your head is three-quarters submerged. Propel yourself by kicking only. Exhale into the water and rotate your head slightly upward to inhale. Concentrate on keeping your hips and legs high. Swim one length and then switch sides. This drill promotes proper technique at maximum rotation.

- **Layout freestyle.** Start by kicking on your side in the manner just described. After 3 to 5 seconds, rotate onto your belly, and catch up to your forward arm with the other arm so that both arms are extended in front of you. Immediately perform a complete pull with the original leading arm and simultaneously rotate onto your other side. Kick for 3 to 5 seconds, and then catch up and rotate once more. After swimming two to four lengths in this way, reduce the amount of time you spend on each side to just 2 seconds. This drill improves body position and rotation.

- **Catch-up freestyle.** Begin by kicking facedown with both arms extended in front of you. After 3 or 4 seconds, perform a complete pull with one arm and rotate fully to that side. Immediately rotate back onto your belly, and catch up to the forward arm with the arm that just pulled. Kick for 3 or 4 seconds, and then pull with the other arm and rotate. Swim two to four lengths in this manner, and then reduce the amount of time you kick on your belly to just 1 second between pulls. Swim two to four lengths more, and then pull twice with each arm before switching sides. This drill promotes better rotation and arm-stroke mechanics.

WORKOUTS: As with the other disciplines discussed in this chapter, in swimming, the appropriate format for active-recovery workouts is 20 to 60 minutes at a steady pace and a low-to-moderate level of intensity. Most of this swimming should be performed freestyle, but some should take the form of the technique drills I've described. A single active-recovery swim per week will suffice for most runners, but there's no harm in swimming more often. When you're injured, again, perform swim workouts that mimic the format of the run workouts you would be doing if you were healthy. Monitoring intensity is best done by feel, as there's no practical way to monitor your heart rate while you swim—you can do it only during breaks between swim intervals.

CROSS-COUNTRY SKIING

ADVANTAGES: Cross-country skiing is just about the only sport that is more physiologically intense than running. At any given effort level, skiing involves more muscle and therefore requires more oxygen than running. So runners who cross-country ski can potentially increase their aerobic capacity and improve their running. Cross-country skiing is also a great way to enhance strength in the hips, quadriceps, abdomen, and shoulders, thereby improving running economy and stride power as well as reducing susceptibility to some overuse injuries.

DISADVANTAGE: There is an obvious difference between cross-country skiing and the other forms of endurance cross-training I've discussed: It's strictly seasonal. For this reason, I think cross-training is best used the way Libbie Hickman used it in her professional running career (and the way I used it during my high school days in New Hampshire): as a fun way to stay in shape during the winter off-season, when you're not in formal training for an upcoming event.

EQUIPMENT: The good news for novice cross-country skiers is that the technology of boots and bindings has made great advances in the past several years, becoming much more stable and hence beginner-friendly. You can rent the very latest and greatest skis and boots at most resorts, where competent professionals can match you with the most appropriate gear and then teach you how to use it. I recommend that you test equipment in this way before buying it. Standard weekend rental fees are in the range of $50 at most resorts. You can purchase a good entry-level package of skis, boots, and poles for around $300.

Proper dress for cross-country skiing includes a moisture-wicking base layer (top and bottom) and socks, a fleece vest, wind pants, a windbreaker, and a polypropylene hat and gloves. You can always remove layers as you heat up.

TECHNIQUE: There are two distinct styles of cross-country skiing: classic and skating. The classic style, also known as kick and glide, involves straight-ahead gliding, as though your skis were on rails. The skating motion is similar to ice-skating or inline skating. Both require balance and coordination, but not so much that the average person cannot master the techniques after two or three lessons. As a beginner, it's best to practice on a smooth, flat surface, such as a snowed-over soccer field. As you advance, you can attack more varied terrain and even go "back country"—that is, create your own trails.

WORKOUTS: There's little need to perform structured workouts on skis, since it's mainly an off-season activity. The best thing about cross-country skiing is that it's a truly exhilarating way to enjoy the outdoors. Concentrate on approaching it as such, and the conditioning aspect will take care of itself. You can do all-day adventures like Libbie Hickman or quick, 45-minute jaunts as I did back when I lived where I could reliably expect to find a base of snow right outside my door during certain months of the year. You can do no running and all skiing for a while, or just ski here and there while continuing to run regularly. You can wear a heart rate monitor to control your intensity or go by feel. In any case, when the snow melts, you'll be in great shape.

There are, of course, cross-country ski machines that can give you the same benefits even after the snow melts. Indoor skiing is as effective as any other activity for active recovery, rehabilitation, and rounding out running fitness. The only reason I choose not to place it higher on the list of recommended endurance cross-training activities for runners is that few fitness clubs have ski simulators, and purchasing one for the home will set you back $600 or more.

THE RUNNING FOUNDATION

NO MATTER HOW GREAT A ROLE cross-training plays in your workout program, running must remain the foundation of your training if you wish to realize your full potential in the sport. As the great running coach Joe Vigil once said to me, "Liberace didn't become a great pianist by chopping wood."

There are four basic ways to improve as a runner, all of which relate to energy. In this chapter, I'll first describe each of these four ways to turn energy to your greater advantage and then talk about how to train for these desired effects. Don't worry about memorizing all the finer points of physiology I present here; just grab the main points, unless you have a special interest in this type of knowledge. Having a solid basic understanding of what running fitness is all about will allow you to make more informed training decisions, as every self-coached runner must to enjoy progress over the long term.

FOUR WAYS TO IMPROVE

Let's employ a race car metaphor to discuss the four fundamental ways to run faster.

1. BUILD A BIGGER ENGINE. The most potent means of getting faster is to increase the rate at which your body is able to produce energy over a full race distance. The more energy your body can generate for forward motion, the faster you will be able to run throughout the race.

The most important physiological attribute underlying the capacity to produce energy at a high rate for a long period of time is aerobic capacity, or VO_2 max—that is, the ability to deliver oxygen to the working muscles. There is a very strong correlation between aerobic capacity and distance-running ability. Here's why.

Unlike a race car, which contains one engine and uses a single fuel type, the human body has two energy systems: aerobic and anaerobic. (Actually, there are three distinct anaerobic energy pathways, but since two of them combined are able to supply energy for only about 18 seconds of maximum-intensity action, we endurance athletes can more or less ignore them.) The aerobic system, used mainly for sustained actions of low-to-moderate intensity, requires oxygen to function. The anaerobic system (specifically anaerobic glycolysis), used mainly for high-intensity actions, does not involve oxygen. The aerobic system produces harmless by-products (carbon dioxide, water, and heat). The anaerobic system produces pyruvate, some of which turns into lactic acid. Lactic acid in turn breaks down into lactate and hydrogen ions that inhibit muscle contractions, cause pain, and perhaps even damage muscle tissues. This is why you can't sprint or lift heavy weights for more than a few dozen seconds before reaching exhaustion.

Contrary to popular belief, whenever you run, at any speed, both the aerobic and anaerobic systems produce energy. When you run slowly, nearly all your energy is produced aerobically. As you speed up and burn more and more total energy, the anaerobic system is required to make larger and larger contributions. However, the faster your body is able to deliver oxygen to the working muscles, the more energy your aerobic system can produce on its own, and the faster you can go before hydrogen ions begin to build up and hasten exhaustion. Also, the aerobic system actually uses pyruvate for energy, thereby preventing lactic acid and hydrogen ions from forming in the first place. So the key to being able to produce energy at a higher rate over a full race distance is to produce more energy aerobically.

Many of the physiological variables underlying aerobic capacity can be positively affected by training. Training enlarges and strengthens the heart so that it can pump more blood and deliver more oxygen per contraction. Training also increases blood plasma volume and hemoglobin content, allowing the blood to carry more oxygen per unit volume. It activates new capillaries that deliver oxygen from the bloodstream to the muscles, and within muscle cells it increases the number of mitochondria, the structures that are the actual site of aerobic metabolism, as well as aerobic enzymes that break down fuel for energy.

2. IMPROVE YOUR FUEL ECONOMY. A second way to improve your running is to reduce the rate at which your body consumes energy at any given velocity of running. The less energy your body actually burns during running, the faster you can go before reaching the maximum speed (maximum rate of energy consumption) you can sustain to the finish line.

In race cars, better fuel economy is achieved mainly through aerodynamics. In runners, there are other factors. The most obvious one is lightness. The less body weight you have to lift and push forward with each stride, the less energy is required to run at any given pace. A runner weighing 160 pounds burns about 6.5 percent more energy than a runner weighing 150 pounds when both run at the same pace. A second factor that affects the energy cost of running is technique. Overpronating at the ankles, striking heel first, wobbling at the knees, and tensing the arms all burn extra energy. There is a neuromuscular component to energy economy as well. Through training, the brain is able to improve the efficiency with which it stimulates the patterns of muscle contractions involved in running. In fact, physiologists now believe that the initial gains in fitness that are seen in the first weeks of running are due primarily to improvements in neuromuscular efficiency.

Also relevant are the proportions of fuel types you burn. The two main fuels for aerobic metabolism are fat and carbohydrate. At lower exercise intensities, fat is burned preferentially because the body has far greater stores of it. The average runner has enough stored fat to run for several days straight. At higher intensities, carbohydrate is preferred because the muscle cells can metabolize it more quickly. However, the body contains enough carbohydrate to fuel only a couple of hours of running at a moderately high intensity. Training can increase your ability to burn fat quickly and at higher intensities, thereby increasing your general endurance.

3. CARRY A BIGGER GAS TANK. The farther you run, the more important fuel storage—specifically carbohydrate fuel storage—becomes. Since carbohydrate is a more efficient fuel than fat for aerobic metabolism, it is always the body's preferred energy source in races. The body stores carbohydrate in relatively small amounts, however, so depletion of carbohydrate fuel is usually the factor that limits your range.

(*continued on page 143*)

TRAINING THE STRIDE

Improving stride mechanics is one of the best ways to improve running economy. But it's a tricky business. There's no single method that does the job completely. The first step (so to speak) is to develop a good understanding of the characteristics of good running form. They are as follows:

High stride rate. Faster runners tend to have a high natural stride rate—about 180 strides per minute at race intensity—and tend to be most efficient at a high stride rate.

Quick footstrikes. Faster runners spend less time in contact with the ground. Two factors that lead to longer footstrikes are overpronation and heel striking (see the next point).

Midfoot- or forefoot-strike. Faster runners tend to land on the midfoot or forefoot rather than on the heel. Heel striking is inefficient for three reasons: (1) It results in more ground-contact time, (2) it has a braking effect, and (3) it corresponds to a lower stride rate because it results from a tendency to take excessively long strides—to overreach with the leading leg.

Large stride angle. Stride length is a function of stride angle—that is, the largest angle that your two thighs form when you're in full stride. Maximum stride angle, in turn, is a function of dynamic flexibility. Faster runners tend to take shorter strides than slower runners at any given pace, which explains why they tend to have a higher stride rate. However, they're also generally *capable* of taking longer strides than slower runners. The larger the strides you can take while maintaining a high, efficient stride rate, the faster you can run.

High kick. Faster runners tend to bend their trailing leg sharply so that the foot comes up high during the recovery (forward-swinging) phase of the stride. Slower runners tend to bend the recovering leg less, resulting in a more shufflelike gait. Physics tells us that swinging a short pendulum requires less energy than swinging a longer one of equal mass, so the high kick is more efficient. A high kick is mostly a passive result of a powerful forward thigh drive.

Minimal vertical motion. Faster runners run forward instead of bouncing. All vertical motion is wasted in running—it literally gets you nowhere.

Neutral posture. Faster runners do not tilt laterally at the hips or forward (the classic "seated runner" look). Nor do they hunch their backs, lean more than a few degrees forward from the pelvis, or twist their torsos excessively from side to side. All of these deviations from neutral posture decrease efficiency.

Relaxed upper body. Faster runners run with loose hands and a long neck or relaxed shoulders. Any unnecessary tension in the upper body wastes energy.

Improving running mechanics is seldom as simple as forcing yourself to, say, run with a high kick. This is because runners tend to naturally find the gait pattern in which they are most efficient *given their present strength and flexibility characteristics*. In order to gain efficiency in running with more correct form, certain muscles will have to become stronger, others more elastic, and so forth. This takes time and a multidimensional approach. Here are eight things you can do to run more like the fastest runners.

1. Watch yourself. Run on a treadmill in view of a full-length mirror and compare your running form against the characteristics of good form. Note the flaws in your technique, and begin the process of correcting them. Even though most common flaws cannot be corrected through a simple act of will, it still pays to diagnose your weaknesses.

2. Be watched. Even better than running in front of a mirror is having a veteran runner, a coach, or an expert on the running stride (perhaps a podiatrist or physical therapist who treats runners) watch you run and point out irregularities.

3. Stretch and strengthen your muscles. In order to correct most form problems, you need to change some muscles—strengthen some, lengthen others, and make others strong through a greater range of motion. This is the main reason you can seldom improve your stride through a conscious act of will alone. Conscious form changes get the process started, but you also need to develop a body that is more

(continued)

TRAINING THE STRIDE *(cont.)*

capable of running efficiently. Strength training and flexibility work can help you do this.

4. Run fast. Running faster tends to lengthen the stride, increase kick height, produce a more forward footstrike, reduce bounce, and increase efficiency at faster cadences. Indeed, I believe fast running is the single most effective way to improve running technique.

5. Develop body awareness. Get in the habit of paying attention to your stride and its various components when you run—especially when you run hard. Do not force changes, but do play with your form a bit to get a sense of how a faster cadence or a midfoot-strike feels. As you continue to do some fast running, stretching, and functional strength training, you'll find that the characteristics of good running form begin to feel increasingly natural. Though running efficiently is impossible without the physical tools, developing good body awareness guides and thereby accelerates the changes that your training makes possible.

6. Wear the right shoes, and use orthotics if you need them. Some form flaws begin with the feet. The bad news is that strength training, stretching, and body awareness can do little to correct foot problems. The good news is that the right equipment can do a lot to correct foot-related flaws—and can do it instantly. For example, by switching to a motion-control shoe or getting fit for orthotics, a severe overpronator can experience an immediate improvement in ground-contact time and consequently in stride rate.

7. Learn to run relaxed. Most runners carry a lot of unnecessary tension when they run, especially in the upper body and when fatigued. Use your body awareness to let go of this tension. This is especially helpful during your high-intensity workouts, when relaxing is most difficult.

8. Practice breathing. Although invisible, breathing is a tremendously important component of the running stride. Correct breathing is controlled and deep but not artificially slowed or exaggerated, and it originates from the diaphragm. Practice breathing in this way, particularly when you run hard. Relaxing and breathing are the two elements of running that respond most readily to conscious mental fiddling.

The capacity to delay exhaustion comes mainly through better carbohydrate conservation and storage. As mentioned, by doing workouts at moderate-to—moderately high intensities, you can train your body to burn more fat during running, including race-pace running. By doing long workouts that deplete carbohydrate stores, you can also train your body to store far greater amounts of carbohydrate. These long workouts are especially important when training for races of half-marathon distance and beyond.

Fortunately, you don't have to rely strictly on stored carbohydrate. While running, you can consume carbohydrate in sports drinks or energy gels, thereby significantly increasing your endurance. The average runner can process ingested carbohydrate at a maximum rate of about 60 to 80 grams per hour during running. This is not nearly enough to offset carbohydrate burning, but it makes a difference. While physiologists doubt whether athletes can increase their capacity to absorb ingested carbohydrate during exercise, it is possible to increase your ability to drink consistently throughout a run without discomfort. So it's important to practice drinking in training.

4. CREATE A BETTER EXHAUST SYSTEM. The runner's "exhaust system" is often undervalued. As mentioned, during running, both the aerobic and anaerobic systems produce energy. The by-products of aerobic metabolism are harmless and easily dealt with. But the hydrogen ions that are produced with lactate by the anaerobic system will do nothing less than shut down the working muscles if allowed to accumulate in them. Again, maximizing aerobic capacity is the best way to minimize this problem, called acidosis, because the more energy you can produce aerobically, the less you have to produce anaerobically.

You can also train to improve your body's ability to deal with lactate and hydrogen ions once they are produced. The body produces lactate buffers (mainly bicarbonate) that neutralize a portion of the lactate. Training—especially high-intensity interval training—increases the effectiveness of these buffers. The body also produces lactate transporters that are responsible for shuttling lactate and hydrogen ions away from the muscles that produce them. (Much of the shuttled lactate goes to the liver, where it is turned back into glycogen.) Training increases the effectiveness of the lactate shuttling system as well. Together, the lactate buffers and transporters constitute your exhaust system with respect to the by-products of anaerobic metabolism. Physiologists believe that improvements in running fitness and performance have more to do with a greater ability to handle these by-products than with reduced production of them.

THE IMPORTANCE OF INTENSITY

The three fundamental training variables are frequency, intensity, and duration. These are the keys to building a bigger engine, increasing your fuel economy, carrying a bigger gas tank, and creating a better exhaust system. Training is nothing more than a game of manipulating these three variables in just the right ways over a period of time leading up to a peak race.

While all three variables are important, the most significant is intensity, formally defined as the rate at which energy is produced relative to the maximum rate at which a given runner can produce it. Informally, intensity is simply how hard you're running at any given time. How hard you run is the primary determinant of how your body adapts to training. The more time you spend running at a certain intensity—that is, the greater the frequency and duration of that intensity—the more your body will tend to change in ways that make it better suited to run at that intensity.

So you see how the three variables together relate to the conditioning process. Generally, intensity determines the nature of the physical changes, while duration and frequency determine the degree. It sounds quite simple—until you look at intensity more closely. When you get down to deciding when and how much to train at various intensities, things are not so clear. First of all, the range of intensities is infinite. For any given runner, there is an intensity associated with 7:00-per-mile pace, an ever-so-slightly different intensity associated with 6:59.5-per-mile pace, another one corresponding to 6:59-per-mile pace—you get the idea. This makes training by intensity inherently imprecise. Further, there is still quite a lot we don't know about the conditioning effects of different exercise intensities. For example, there is a popular belief that running at the anaerobic threshold is the most effective way to elevate this threshold, but it's still unclear whether this is actually (or always) the case. Consequently, deciding when and how much to train at various intensity levels always involves guesswork.

The best guidelines we have for manipulating training intensity come from the evolution of run training. Over the decades, runners and their coaches have tried just about everything. Certain ideas and practices have borne little fruit, while others have repeatedly proven themselves effective. As a result, better running coaches and better-informed runners exhibit a fairly standardized approach to training by intensity. Here are four golden rules of intensity that have emerged from the evolution of run training.

1. **CERTAIN WORKOUTS JUST PLAIN WORK.** There is a tendency in some quarters to overlook the fact that you can train very effectively without having the slightest idea why the training is working or what's going on inside your body. Many years of collective trial and error have yielded an array of standard workout formats that, when performed in the right order and in the right proportions, produce reliable gains in fitness. These classic formats represent optimal ways to train at each of the six intensity levels or ranges that I will discuss in detail.

2. **MOST RUNNING SHOULD BE RELATIVELY SLOW.** History has shown that the best results come when you consistently perform 80 to 90 percent of your running at lower intensities. Attempts to handle greater amounts of high-intensity training almost always result in stagnation or injury. This is why distance runners do not always train at a full sprint: The faster you run, the less you can run without becoming worn down or injured. Doing most of your running at a comfortable pace enables you to do more total running and thus experience greater overall adaptations. Though it may seem counterintuitive, doing a goodly amount of slower running conditions you to handle more fast running.

3. **GRADUAL PROGRESSION TO HIGH-INTENSITY RUNNING WORKS BEST.** Don't get me wrong: High-intensity training is good—so good, in fact, that during certain portions of the training process, you should perform as much of it as you can handle. It's just that the amount of running at high intensity any runner can handle is very small compared to the feasible amount of running at low-to-moderate intensity. Beginning runners should perform little hard running at first and gradually increase the amount until they reach their personal limit. Fitter and more experienced runners who can handle the most hard running should nevertheless begin each new period of training with no more than a small amount of hard running.

4. **EACH RUNNER IS UNIQUE.** Individual runners respond to similar training in different ways. This is why training methods have not yet nor ever will become completely uniform. Your running career should be an

ongoing quest to find your best training practices. Start with a sensible program based on tried-and-true methods. Analyze the results and use them to create a refined program to train for your next big event. Repeat this process in each new period of training.

TARGET INTENSITIES

There are six intensity levels that you should target in your training. Each stimulates a set of adaptations that is different (if only slightly, in the case of some "neighboring" target intensities) from the set of adaptations associated with any other intensity. Each run you do should focus on one, or at most two, of the six.

RECOVERY. In trained runners, recovery intensity corresponds to 55 to 65 percent of VO_2 max. The rate of carbohydrate metabolism is equal to or just slightly higher than that of fat metabolism. Blood lactate levels generally do not rise or rise very little above resting levels in trained runners working at recovery intensity. Initial perceived effort on a 1-to-10 scale is between 4 and 5. (I refer to "initial perceived effort" instead of just "perceived effort," as others do, because perceived effort climbs at any intensity level if it is maintained long enough for fatigue to set in. Recovery pace corresponds to ultra-marathon race pace, and after 95 miles of running at this pace, you can bet your perceived effort level will be 10 or close to it.)

The primary purpose of running at recovery intensity is to promote recovery from recent hard training. The standard workout format for recovery-intensity training is the recovery run: 20 to 60 minutes, slow and steady.

MODERATE AEROBIC. Moderate-aerobic running is slightly more intense than recovery running. It corresponds to 65 to 75 percent of VO_2 max in trained runners. Energy comes predominantly from carbohydrate, but a fair amount of fat is still being metabolized. Blood lactate levels are stable but above resting levels. Initial perceived effort is 5 to 6.

There are two standard workout formats for moderate-aerobic running.

1. What I call a *foundation run* consists of 30 to 90 minutes of steady running. Foundation runs are used to build a general base of aerobic fitness early in the training process and to maintain aerobic fitness later on.

2. A *long run* is simply a longer version (90 to 180 minutes) of a foundation run. Long runs are used to increase endurance.

HIGH AEROBIC. High-aerobic running ranges between roughly 10 percent slower than marathon race pace on the low end and marathon race pace on the high end. In a typical fit runner, this range corresponds to 75 to 85 percent of VO_2 max. Carbohydrate provides all or virtually all of the energy for muscle contractions. Initial perceived effort is 6 to 7. High-aerobic running is most appropriate for foundation runs in the late base-building period of training and for long runs and marathon-pace runs in the latter period of half-marathon and marathon training.

ANAEROBIC THRESHOLD. In a typical well-trained runner, the anaerobic threshold falls between 85 and 90 percent of VO_2 max. Blood lactate is at the maximum steady-state level; if the pace were increased even slightly from here, the blood lactate level would climb and keep climbing, eventually causing exhaustion. Initial perceived effort is about 8.

Anaerobic threshold is the appropriate target intensity for tempo runs, which consist of 20 to 40 minutes of hard but controlled running between an easy warmup and a cooldown. In cruise-interval workouts, a tempo run is broken into two or three segments of harder running with recovery-intensity running between them.

AEROBIC CAPACITY. Aerobic capacity, or VO_2 max, is the maximum rate of oxygen consumption a runner can achieve while running. In most trained runners, this rate of oxygen consumption is reached after a few minutes of running at the fastest pace that can be maintained for 5 to 8 minutes. This pace corresponds to an initial perceived effort of 9. Training at aerobic capacity is a good way to increase VO_2 max, to improve running economy, and to strengthen the lactate buffering and shuttling capacities.

The standard workout format for training at this intensity is a set of four to six hard intervals lasting 3 to 4 minutes apiece, with a few minutes of recovery jogging between them.

SPEED. Speed intensity is anything above VO_2 max intensity and below a full sprint—in other words, between 600m and 1500m race pace. Middle-distance runners benefit from a small amount of sprinting, but distance runners need not ever run 100 percent full-tilt in training. Speed-intensity running exceeds 100 percent of VO_2 max, which means runners are in a state of oxygen deficit when running this fast. Initial perceived effort at

PAULA RADCLIFFE

Paula Radcliffe is so good that she could almost make the British men's Olympic team. When she won the 2003 London Marathon in a time of 2:15:25, Radcliffe was the first British finisher, male or female (and the 15th finisher overall). With that performance, she also brought the women's marathon world record within 10 minutes of the men's record for the first time in history.

Radcliffe first showed her promise on the international stage with a victory in the 1992 World Junior Cross-Country Championships. She has since won two senior World Cross-Country Championships titles and three World Half-Marathon Championships. In addition to having twice set the marathon world record, she also holds world records in the road 5-K (14:51) and road 10-K (30:21) and a world best performance in the half-marathon (1:05:41).

Coached by her husband, a former elite miler, Radcliffe trains mostly on her own and has gradually developed a training system that is well-customized to her strengths and needs. It features high mileage, a lot of high-aerobic running, heavy reliance on hill training in the winter, and 1 day of rest every 8 days.

She has training bases outside the U.K. in Albuquerque, New Mexico, and in the resort town of Font Romeu, France. While there, when conditions permit, she does a 45-minute recovery workout on cross-country skis every week. When snow is unavailable, she does the same workout on an indoor cross-country ski machine to get a little more aerobic stimulus without subjecting her legs to more impact forces. Radcliffe has said that she prefers cross-country skiing because she feels it is the nonimpact activity that most closely approximates the feeling of running and because it strengthens the core muscles of the stomach and lower back. Perhaps Britain's male marathoners ought to try it!

speed intensity is between 9 and 10. Training at this intensity level increases VO$_2$ max and develops fast-twitch muscle fibers.

There are two standard ways to train at speed intensity. One is a set of several short, hard intervals with jogging recoveries. For example, 12 400m runs with 3-minute jogging recoveries. The other way, good for small doses of speed intensity, is "strides." These consist of sets of 4 to 10 hard runs of about 100 yards each, separated by recovery jogs and performed after an easy run.

CONTROLLING INTENSITY

Pace is the most convenient and useful means of measuring and controlling your running intensity. Each of the target intensities just described corresponds to a particular pace or pace range in an individual runner (assuming standardized conditions such as level terrain and weather). These pace levels increase gradually as fitness increases. All you need in order to monitor the pace of running is a stopwatch and a measured course, such as a 400m track. In fact, nowadays you don't even need the latter. A device like the Timex Speed-Distance system, which uses GPS technology, allows you to track the distance you've run to the thousandth of a mile in real time anywhere on earth.

Most runners use pace to measure the intensity of running but not to control the intensity. The difficulty is that pace in itself does not indicate the physiological states that truly represent intensity. Pace alone, for example, cannot be used to determine whether or not you are running at aerobic capacity. However, there is, as I suggested above, a pace or pace range that corresponds to each real physiological intensity state in an individual runner. These pace levels can be determined through a treadmill test in which your VO$_2$ and blood lactate levels are measured at various paces.

The fact that this type of testing has already been done with thousands of other runners allows you to skip it. Distance runners who achieve similar times in races also tend to have about the same lactate thresholds and aerobic-capacity paces, as determined through laboratory testing. Since these variables are the most direct indicators of appropriate target intensities, it follows that runners who race at the same pace as one another should also train at about the same pace in all types of workout.

(continued on page 152)

PACE AT A GIVEN INTENSITY LEVEL

10-K RACE TIME	RECOVERY PACE (PER MILE)	MODERATE-AEROBIC PACE (PER MILE)	HIGH-AEROBIC PACE (PER MILE)	ANAEROBIC-THRESHOLD PACE (PER MILE)	AEROBIC-CAPACITY PACE (PER 400M)	SPEED PACE (PER 400M)
1:03:46	12:43	12:16	11:02	10:18	2:22	2:16
1:02:03	12:25	11:59	11:02	10:03	2:18	2:12
1:00:26	12:07	11:41	10:29	9:47	2:14	2:08
58:54	11:51	11:25	10:15	9:34	2:11	2:05
57:26	11:30	11:09	10:00	9:20	2:08	2:02
56:03	11:21	10:55	9:47	9:08	2:05	1:59
54:44	11:05	10:40	9:33	8:55	2:02	1:55
53:29	10:52	10:27	9:21	8:44	1:59	1:53
52:17	10:39	10:14	9:08	8:33	1:56	1:50
51:09	10:27	10:02	8:57	8:23	1:54	1:48
50:03	10:15	9:50	8:46	8:12	1:52	1:46
49:01	10:04	9:39	8:36	8:02	1:50	1:44
48:01	9:52	9:28	8:25	7:52	1:48	1:42
47:04	9:42	9:18	8:16	7:43	1:46	1:40
46:09	9:31	9:07	8:06	7:33	1:44	1:38
45:16	9:22	8:58	7:57	7:25	1:42	1:36
44:25	9:12	8:48	7:48	7:17	1:40	1:34
43:36	9:02	8:39	7:40	7:10	1:38	1:32
42:50	8:53	8:31	7:32	7:02	1:36	1:30
42:04	8:45	8:22	7:24	6:55	1:35	1:29
41:21	8:37	8:14	7:17	6:51	1:33	1:27
40:39	8:30	8:07	7:09	6:44	1:32	1:26
39:59	8:21	7:59	7:02	6:38	1:31	1:25
39:20	8:14	7:52	6:56	6:32	1:30	1:24

10-K RACE TIME	RECOVERY PACE (PER MILE)	MODERATE-AEROBIC PACE (PER MILE)	HIGH-AEROBIC PACE (PER MILE)	ANAEROBIC-THRESHOLD PACE (PER MILE)	AEROBIC-CAPACITY PACE (PER 400M)	SPEED PACE (PER 400M)
38:42	8:07	7:45	6:49	6:26	1:28	1:22
38:06	8:00	7:38	6:43	6:20	1:27	1:21
37:31	7:53	7:31	6:37	6:15	1:26	1:20
36:57	7:46	7:25	6:31	6:09	1:25	1:19
36:24	7:40	7:19	6:25	6:04	1:23	1:17
35:52	7:34	7:13	6:19	5:59	1:22	1:16
35:22	7:28	7:07	6:14	5:54	1:21	1:15
34:52	7:21	7:01	6:09	5:50	1:20	1:14
34:23	7:16	6:56	6:04	5:45	1:19	1:13
33:55	7:10	6:50	5:59	5:41	1:18	1:12
33:28	7:05	6:45	5:54	5:36	1:17	1:11
33:01	6:59	6:40	5:49	5:32	1:16	1:10
32:35	6:54	6:35	5:45	5:28	1:15	1:09
32:11	6:48	6:30	5:40	5:24	1:14	1:08
31:46	6:44	6:26	5:36	5:20	1:13	1:07
31:23	6:39	6:21	5:32	5:16	1:12	1:06
31:00	6:35	6:17	5:28	5:13	1:11	1:05
30:38	6:29	6:12	5:24	5:09	1:10	1:04
30:16	6:25	6:08	5:20	5:05	1:09	1:03
29:55	6:21	6:04	5:16	5:02	1:09	1:02
29:34	6:16	6:00	5:12	4:59	1:08	1:02
29:14	6:12	5:56	5:09	4:56	1:07	1:01
28:55	6:08	5:52	5:05	4:52	1:06	1:00
28:36	6:03	5:48	5:01	4:49	1:05	0:59
28:17	6:00	5:45	4:58	4:46	1:05	0:59
27:59	5:56	5:41	4:55	4:43	1:04	0:58

The legendary running coach and exercise physiologist Jack Daniels has taken this insight the furthest. Using the pace-physiology relationship, he created a complete system that allows individual runners to determine the appropriate pace for each type of workout based on a recent race performance. I have modified this system just slightly in the table "Pace at a Given Intensity Level" on the preceding pages.

Here's how it works. After you've built a solid training base but before you begin doing high-intensity workouts, run a 10-K test race or run a timed 10-K on the track. Then look on the table to find the 10-K time that's closest to yours. The numbers in the columns to the right of that time are your recommended pace levels for each of the six target intensities. If your 10-K time falls between two adjacent times in the left column, average the paces in these two rows in each of the six columns to the right. In any case, these pace levels are both approximate and initial. If you do an appropriately structured workout at the suggested pace and it feels too hard or too easy, slow down or speed up a bit. And expect your pace at any given intensity level to increase gradually as you become fitter.

Although the table provides a single, specific pace for the recovery, moderate-aerobic, and high-aerobic intensity levels, each is truly intended to represent a point within a range. The number in the high-aerobic column is your approximate marathon pace. The numbers in the anaerobic-threshold, aerobic-capacity, and speed columns should be right on the money or very close.

Some experienced runners might even be able to skip the test 10-K. If you've done your share of road races, you probably know how fast you could run a 10-K today, and you can use that time instead. Just don't let your ego influence your estimate unduly!

TRAINING PROGRAMMATICALLY

How do you combine individual run workouts at target intensities into a program that gets you into peak shape for your next important race? The simplest way is to be guided by three basic principles: progressive overload, specific adaptation, and optimal recovery.

PROGRESSIVE OVERLOAD. Systems of the body adapt best when they are required to do just a little more than they are accustomed to doing. When they are required to do too much too soon, maladaptation (some form of breakdown) is inevitable. On the other hand, when body systems are not continuously slightly overloaded, adaptation ceases altogether, or worse, reverse adaptation (also known as detraining) begins. The principle of progressive overload is manifest in the following training practices.

1. **Begin each new training period with a relatively low volume of training and increase it gradually.**

2. **Introduce each new type of workout into the training program with a relatively moderate version thereof, and increase its challenge gradually from one session to the next.**

3. **Increase the overall training workload very gradually from one year to the next, until an appropriate "career maximum" workload is reached.** The adaptations your body undergoes during the present period of training allow you not only to race faster at the end of it but also to train harder in the next period of training.

SPECIFIC ADAPTATION. The body adapts very specifically in response to the precise nature of the demands that are placed upon it in training. The objective of training is to stimulate the specific adaptations that are needed to allow you to achieve your race goals. The following training patterns are most reliable in this regard.

1. **Perform a wide variety of workout types, each of which is designed to stimulate specific needed adaptations.** With this approach, you can achieve a "surplus" of each adaptation. For example, doing long runs that are longer (at least in duration) than races creates a surplus of endurance. Likewise, running intervals faster than race pace creates a surplus of speed (actually muscle-fiber recruitment capacity). Doing both of these types of training will therefore enable you to race faster than you could if you never exceeded race duration or race pace in training. This principle is also the justification for practices such as strength training (surplus strength) and stretching (surplus mobility).

2. **Divide training into distinct phases wherein different types of training are emphasized.** The most race-specific types of workouts should be emphasized in the final weeks before a peak race. For a runner training for a marathon, these would be long runs, marathon-pace runs, and tempo runs. Before the race-specific training is emphasized, it's best to emphasize different types of training that will prepare you for

peak-level training. This includes a fair amount of running at faster than race pace.

3. Perform a gradually increasing volume of mostly moderate-aerobic-intensity running in the early part of training. This prepares you to handle much harder workouts later. As a general rule, and up to a point, the more easy running you do early in the training period, the more hard running you can do later.

OPTIMAL RECOVERY. Fitness does not increase during workouts, for the most part. It increases *between* workouts, during the recovery process, as various systems of the body respond and adapt to the stresses imposed on them during workouts. There's a difference between training and absorbing training. What matters is not how much good training you do but how much good training you actually absorb through recovery. Any training you do that is not absorbed will more likely diminish than enhance your fitness. The principle of optimal recovery is manifest in the following training practices.

1. Practice step cycles. These are recurring patterns of training that last 2 to 4 weeks and end with a week of reduced-volume training for recovery. In a 2-week step cycle, a week of hard training is followed by a week of lighter training. In a 3-week cycle, the first week is relatively hard, the second week slightly harder, and the third week easy. In a 4-week cycle, the third week of training is slightly harder than the second. Planning recovery periods into your training in this way helps ensure that you don't accumulate fatigue during a long training program. It also makes the fitness-building process more gradual, and the more gradually you build toward a fitness peak, the higher that peak will be when you get there.

2. Deliberately "undertrain." The best race results come when you have *fully absorbed* the maximum amount of specific, progressive training your body can absorb. The only trouble is that locating this limit can be tricky, and the consequences of transgressing it by even a little bit can be grave from a performance perspective. You'll almost certainly race better after having done 10 percent less training than you could have absorbed than after having done just 5 percent too much. So you should always plan a training workload that, based on your self-knowledge, is close to your perceived absorption limit but squarely on the safe side of it.

3. Practice responsive training. By responsive training, I mean making adjustments to your training plan as you go, in response to the results of the training you've done thus far—and particularly in response to your present recovery status. Go easier than planned when you feel you need to, and don't be afraid to go hard when you feel ready. Schedule your tougher workouts in pencil, as they say, and move them back or forward or modify or scratch them as necessary.

4. Taper before races. Cutting way back on your training workload as an important race nears will ensure that you have fully absorbed your recent peak training and are rested and ready for a peak performance.

Those are the principles of training. In the next chapter, I'll show you how to use these principles to create a cross-training-based program for peak running performance.

PUTTING IT ALL TOGETHER

EFFECTIVE TRAINING CALLS FOR a continual oscillation between planning and adjustment. If you don't plan, you'll find it nearly impossible to truly progress. The first requirement for effective planning is a sound understanding of the universal principles and methods of training. But to make the most of your planning, you need to practice three types of adjustment: customization, improvisation, and refinement.

CUSTOMIZATION occurs during the planning process itself and is based on the uniqueness of each runner. Individual runners have different strengths and weaknesses, goals, life schedules, and responses to training. A program that takes these factors into account will be more effective than one that does not. When you customize your training, you essentially take a cookie-cutter, one-size-fits-all training plan based *only* on the universal principles and methods of training and adjust it to make it *really* fit you.

A good example of customization can be found in the better collegiate cross-country programs, in which a collection of runners with similar ability and experience levels train to compete in the same races. The coaches of these teams train each of the runners in slightly (or sometimes even drastically) different ways based on their knowledge of each runner's strengths, weaknesses, injury status, training history, response to training, and even personality. In order to train yourself as well as these scholarship harriers are trained, you need to know and ob-serve yourself as minutely as the top collegiate coaches do their young athletes.

IMPROVISATION happens when you depart from your plan as unex-pected results or circumstances arise. For example, at some point you may find that you are insufficiently recovered from recent training to perform a scheduled key workout. In such a case, you would be better served to replace the key workout with an active-recovery session. If you adhere too stubbornly to the letter of your schedule, you'll frequently fail to do the right thing at the right time in your training, because even the best of plans is nothing more than a collection of educated guesses that cannot foresee the future.

REFINEMENT comes into play once you have completed a peak race and before you begin serious preparations for the next peak. At this time, you reflect on the strengths and flaws of your previous program, assess how you have changed since you began it, and use these observa-tions to create a new and better program to take you to your next goal. For example, perhaps you tried a high-mileage approach in your most re-cent training cycle but found that it caused you to continually teeter on the brink of injury. In planning the next training cycle, you might choose to replace a couple of runs with endurance cross-training workouts each week.

I call this plan-and-adjust approach to training the experimental ap-proach, as this name captures the notions that each runner is unique (an experiment of one), that all planning is necessarily provisional, and that it's always possible to hone and improve one's training over time. My goal in this chapter is to show you how to develop a truly customized cross-training program for running, to adjust it when necessary, and to use what you learn during the process to refine your future training.

THE ART OF PLANNING

If you're a fitness runner who does not participate in races, you don't need planned training programs. You can do more or less the same workouts week in and week out and still enjoy the benefits you seek: weight maintenance, stress reduction, and so forth. Likewise, if you're new to running, you can probably improve steadily for some time without following any kind of formal training plan, as long as you do a sensible amount of training (neither too much nor too little). When your body is only beginning the process of adapting to running, almost any kind of training you do, within reason, will improve your level of adaptation. However, even a beginner will make faster progress by training systematically.

As you become increasingly fit and decide to seek the challenges of racing, a formal, progressive program becomes not just advisable but essential. The whole point of making a training plan is to ensure that you achieve a fitness peak on the day of your next big running event. You should break your training into 12- to 24-week cycles, each leading up to a peak event that establishes the end point of the cycle. A training cycle can be closer to 12 weeks when your initial fitness level is higher, when you are training for a shorter event, and when your goals are modest. It should be closer to 24 weeks when your initial fitness level is lower, when you are training for a longer event, and when your goals are very challenging. The training cycle should always be close to 24 weeks if you are in search of a true peak performance (the best you're capable of at this point in your running life) at the 10-K distance or beyond.

Since most road races take place in the spring and the fall, a sensible annual routine is to start one longer training cycle around the holiday season to culminate with a peak race in the spring, then begin another long cycle culminating in a peak race in the fall, and then take a break. This does not mean that you get to race only twice a year. In the latter portion of each cycle, you may—and indeed should—do other races in addition to your peak race.

This is just one way to plan your training cycles. If you race with a team, for example, you may need to pursue a different kind of schedule. You should always adhere to two rules of scheduling, however. First, always allow at least 12 weeks between peak races. In order to achieve a bona fide fitness peak, you need to complete the three phases of training (base, build, and peak), and you cannot cram them into a time period shorter than 12 weeks. Second, always complete at least one long training cycle (24 weeks or close to it) each year. A fitness peak is highest when it is approached most gradually.

It is always best to plan complete training cycles, each culminating in a peak race, one at a time. Planning more than one at a time takes away the opportunity to use the results of the present plan to make the next one better (refinement).

The best time to plan a training cycle is shortly before you begin it, which in most cases is also shortly after you have completed your most recent cycle. This allows you to build a program that is based on your current fitness level and on the results of your previous cycle. To create a training schedule, complete the following five steps in order: (1) choose a peak race, (2) divide the training cycle into phases and step cycles, (3) establish weekly training-volume goals, (4) select key workouts, and (5) schedule foundation runs and active recoveries. Let's take a close look at each of these steps.

STEP ONE: CHOOSE A PEAK RACE

The nature of your peak race (track 10-K, road marathon, trail ultra-marathon, or what have you) and the goal you attach to it establish the type and volume of training you will perform within a cycle. Which event you choose as your peak race is entirely up to you (unless, again, you compete for a team or belong to a club with a common race agenda). Above all, your chosen peak race should be an event that interests and excites you. It must also be far enough in the future to allow time for adequate preparation.

If your peak race is a short-distance event (10-K or shorter), you may choose to do several other races of the same or similar distance before it. In this case, what distinguishes your peak race from the other races within the training cycle is that the peak race is the only one you will do after having completed the full cycle, including a good taper. Thus, you will probably achieve your best performance in this final race. Generally, your peak race should be the longest race you do, because longer races require more training and more recovery time. It is not hard to run a good 5-K without disrupting your training toward a marathon peak race. It would be very difficult to run a good marathon, or do so without seriously disrupting your training, if you were training toward a 5-K peak race.

It's best not to choose any specific prepeak races you might like to do until you work out the details of your training schedule. This is because your prepeak races must be carefully integrated into the training process to ensure that you both train and race optimally.

The goal that you set for your peak race should be challenging yet attainable. It should take into account your current fitness level, your recent performances, the amount of preparation time you're allowing yourself, and the volume of training you plan to do (and will realistically be able to handle). Setting a goal motivates you to give your best effort. The goals that are most likely to do this are those that you are hopeful but not certain you will be able to achieve. If you do indeed give your best effort, the goal was a good one, regardless of whether you achieved it by the numbers.

Go ahead and register for your peak race as soon as you've chosen it, if you can. Laying down money for a race number is an effective motivational trick. Then waste no time before scheduling the race in whatever you will be using as a training calendar. You can create your schedule on a regular calendar or datebook or on a computer spreadsheet or word processing program. There are even training software programs with bells and whistles, such as PC Coach, and Web sites such as www.trainingbible.com.

You should both schedule and log your training. The difference between a training schedule and a training log (or journal) is that the former records what you plan to do and the latter records what you have actually done. This does not require two separate calendars. Just erase or delete each planned workout as you complete it, and replace it with the details of your actual workout. For each workout, record your distance, your time, your heart rate (if you use a monitor), and a little information about how your body felt. Even just a word like *sluggish* or *zippy* will do. Describe any noteworthy aches and pains as well. This information will help you learn more about the way your body responds to training and about the causes of fatigue or injury. You can also use your training journal to keep track of how many miles you've put on your shoes so that you can replace them on a schedule (every 500 to 600 miles).

STEP TWO: DIVIDE THE TRAINING CYCLE INTO PHASES AND STEP CYCLES

After establishing start and end points for your training cycle, divide it into the three phases: base, build, and peak. (A fourth phase, called transition, falls between training cycles.)

BASE PHASE. The objectives of the first phase of the training cycle are to gradually build aerobic capacity and endurance, to increase your body's ability to absorb running impact, and to begin strengthening the anaerobic system in preparation for the harder training to come. You can achieve the first three objectives by doing nearly all of your running at moderate-aerobic intensity and slowly increasing your weekly running volume and the duration of your longest run. To begin strengthening your anaerobic system, perform a set of strides after two foundation runs per week.

Begin the phase by doing just slightly more running than you have been doing recently. Run by feel: On days when you feel strong, go a little faster or farther; on days when you feel sluggish or tired, run as slowly as you need to in order to feel comfortable. Try a hillier route at least once a week. Your first weekly long run should be just slightly longer than your typical foundation run. Make it 5 percent longer each subsequent week or 10 percent longer every other week.

About every fourth week, reduce your training volume 10 to 20 percent for recovery, then resume the building process. (I will say more about this later in the chapter, in the section on step cycles.) The total length of the base phase, and of the subsequent phases, will depend on your initial fitness level, your goals, and the length of your peak race.

As for cross-training, mix in endurance cross-training workouts according to your needs and preferences and the guidelines I've offered. One active-recovery workout in a nonimpact discipline is the minimum. Do two or three functional strength workouts per week, and stretch consistently.

BUILD PHASE. The objectives of this phase are to further strengthen the aerobic and anaerobic systems, to improve the lactate exhaust system, to optimize economy, and, for less fit runners and runners training for longer races, to further increase endurance. Individual training programs will move in different directions depending on the runner's experience, fitness level, and goals. In general, though, this phase is characterized by a leveling off of training volume and the introduction of high-intensity workouts (anaerobic-threshold intensity and above).

I recommend focusing on speed-intensity workouts in the first part of the build phase, for two reasons. First, they are the best type of workout for increasing your ability to handle heavier training. Second, they are further from race intensity than the other types of high-intensity workout that, as a general rule, you should emphasize later in the training cycle.

In the second half of the build phase, the focus shifts toward aerobic-capacity training (for example, lactate intervals). It's best to do the majority of your aerobic-capacity work at this time because it's very taxing, so you want to have a good level of fitness before you tackle lactate intervals. Doing aerobic-capacity training at this point also allows you to reduce it well before your peak race so that you have time to absorb it. Runners who are willing and able to do two or three high-intensity workouts per week will also do workouts at anaerobic threshold throughout this phase as a secondary training emphasis.

Reduce your training volume for recovery every third or fourth week during this phase, depending on your needs. Continue doing long runs once a week. During the second half of the phase, you can do one or two 5- to 10-K races instead of lactate-interval workouts. Each week, at least one of your active-recovery workouts should be in a nonimpact discipline. Strength-train twice a week, and continue to stretch frequently throughout the phase.

PEAK PHASE. Here, your objectives are to make your fitness as race-specific as possible and to achieve a well-timed fitness peak for the peak race of the training cycle. Emphasize anaerobic-threshold training, because it increases race-specific fitness for every event, from the 10-K distance all the way up to the marathon. Those training for marathons should perform their longest runs during the peak phase, and marathoners with time goals should also do two or three marathon-pace runs. Those who are training for shorter races and who can handle two or three high-intensity workouts per week should do a small amount of work at the aerobic-capacity and speed intensities in addition to their anaerobic-threshold training. Alternatively, they can race more frequently.

The last 1 to 2 weeks of the peak phase should feature very light training. To achieve a true fitness peak prior to an important race, it's essential to drastically reduce training—a strategy called *tapering*. As you taper, keep the proportions of workout types the same (that is, continue doing some high-intensity running), but reduce the duration of all workouts progressively. Do not perform any lower-body strength training in the final week before your peak race.

TRANSITION PHASE. This is the period of informal training that follows a peak race and precedes the next base phase. As such, it falls outside the actual training cycle. Your objectives are to rejuvenate your body and mind and to provide a solid fitness foundation upon which to build in the next training cycle. The transition phase can be any length, depending on your needs. Sometimes you need a good long break from formal training; other times you may find yourself ready to move quickly from one goal to the next.

Cross-training can really help a transition phase serve its objectives by giving you a break from running and by developing your fitness in ways that can complement your running. While your focus should be on endurance activities, this is also the best time to do the most strength training—up to three sessions per week and three sets per exercise.

In most cases, the phases of the training cycle proper—base, build, and peak—should be roughly equal in length. So if you are planning a 12-week cycle, you will want to make each phase last 4 weeks; a 21-week cycle should have three 7-week phases. Outright beginners and those who are starting back after a long layoff will need a longer base phase relative to the other phases. Your base phase can be shorter than the others if you are just coming off a fitness peak and you wish to immediately begin training for another peak race of half-marathon distance or less. But once a year, you should treat yourself to a transition phase of at least 4 weeks, for physical and mental regeneration. Follow this with a longer base phase in order to establish a solid new fitness foundation.

Experienced runners who are starting at a high level of fitness and who are training toward a competitive marathon or half-marathon will benefit from a longer build phase. Middle-distance and 5-K specialists who plan to do a high volume of racing may need to make the peak phase longer than the other two.

In adjusting the relative lengths of the training phases, an even more important factor is the way your body responds to the various intensities of training that are emphasized in each phase. The best way to gauge your body's response is to complete a training cycle with equal-length phases and pay close attention to the way each phase affects you. You will be able to make cause-and-effect connections that you can use in planning your next training cycle. This is a part of the refinement process.

Each phase should be further divided into step cycles—2- to 4-week blocks of training whose purpose is to establish recurring patterns of hard work and recovery that increase your fitness gradually and steadily. In a 2-week step cycle, a week of high-workload training is followed by a reduced-training recovery week. In a 3-week step cycle, the first week is challenging, the second week is more challenging, and the third week is a recovery week. In a 4-week cycle, the third week is the most challenging and the fourth is for recovery.

At this point, don't worry about establishing actual training workloads for each week. Simply decide where you want your recovery weeks to fall. For less experienced runners, I recommend 3-week step cycles (that is, a recovery week every third week) in the base phase, and either 2- or 3-week step cycles in the build and peak phases. Runners with a longer background of consistent training can generally handle 4-week step cycles in the base phase and 3- or 4-week step cycles in the intensity and peak phases.

Of course, it's unlikely that each of the three training phases will be evenly divisible by the length of the step cycles you plan to do. For example, suppose you plan a 6-week base phase and are comfortable with a recovery week every 4 weeks in this phase. You don't need to be John Nash to see that you cannot have it both ways. This is no big deal. The point of this portion of planning is to schedule recovery weeks for the times you think you will need them. It doesn't matter whether all the step cycles in any given phase are the same length. Just do your best to guess when and how often you will need to reduce training in order to absorb recent hard training and prepare for more. If you guess wrong, as all runners do sometimes, this is no big deal, either. You can give yourself an opportunity for recovery whenever you feel you need it during the training process (improvisation). As long as you train hard enough during your hard weeks that you need an occasional recovery week, and you recover enough during these weeks that you're ready for even harder work during the ensuing 1 to 3 weeks, you're doing fine.

Since your racing schedule will affect your recovery needs, now is the time to schedule any and all prepeak races you plan to do. Generally, there is no point in racing until the end of the base phase, at the earliest. Prior to this, you are not fit enough to race well. Doing a low-key race at the end of the base phase can serve as a test, the results of which will help guide your build-phase training, but it is not necessary. Avoid racing during the first half of the build phase, too, since this is the period of maximum overload. If you are challenging yourself as you should be, you will not race well, and racing could all too easily take your body over the edge and into the abyss of overtraining. In the second half of the build phase, you can do one or more shorter races in place of high-intensity workouts and probably see good results. But the majority of your racing should take place in the peak phase, when accumulated fitness and a lighter workload will have you ready to do your best.

It's ideal to schedule races for the end of a recovery week so that you're well-rested for them. Justified exceptions include shorter races that you may wish to do in place of key workouts. It's up to you whether to schedule recovery weeks first and then choose races that happen to take place at accommodating times, or choose your races first and schedule recovery weeks to accommodate them.

There's no formula to determine how often to race. Some runners like to race more often than others, and some benefit from racing more often than others. The shorter your races, the more often you can race, up to a point. I recommend doing at least one prepeak race in each training cycle, because races can be great workouts, will provide experience you can apply to your peak race, can be motivating, and can reward the hard work you do in training. For example, you might very well be able to set a 5-K PR in a prepeak race while training toward setting a 10-K PR at the culmination of your current training cycle.

Racing too often is worse than not racing often enough. Racing too much can interfere with your training, as you need to rest before racing, in order to perform well, and after racing, in order to recover. If you race week after week, you won't be able to get in much quality training beyond what you get in the races themselves. Before long, your fitness will stagnate and your performances will begin to suffer. Similarly, if you try to maintain a normal training schedule despite frequent racing, by limiting prerace rest and postrace recovery, you'll be fatigued for races and workouts alike.

STEP THREE: SET WEEKLY TRAINING-VOLUME GOALS

It's time to decide *how much* training you will do. After dividing the training cycle into phases and scheduling your races and planned recovery weeks, set an approximate training-volume goal for each week of the cycle. Most runners set mileage targets, but since you're cross-training, you should set both a mileage target and a training-hours target for each week. The latter will include all of your running, endurance cross-training, strength training, and flexibility training.

Let's talk about running mileage first. (Naturally, you can measure your running volume in kilometers, rather than miles, if you prefer. You may also measure your running volume in hours and minutes. As long as you're consistent, it really doesn't matter.) In your first week of base training, plan to do about the same amount of running as you did the previous week. If you have not been running, plan to do an amount you know you can easily handle. Increase your running volume by about 10 percent from week to week through the rest of the base phase, except in recovery weeks, when you should cut back by 10 to 20 percent from the previous week.

Throughout the build phase, most runners should maintain relatively consistent total weekly volume while gradually increasing the volume of high-intensity training. Runners training for a marathon generally should continue to increase total running volume in this phase, but not as steadily as in the base phase. A good way to proceed is to perform 3-week step cycles wherein the first week is at roughly the highest volume level you achieved in the base phase, the second week is slightly higher (5 to 10 percent) in volume than any preceding week, and the third week is lower (10 to 20 percent) in volume, for recovery. Each subsequent step cycle should then start at a volume between those of the first and second weeks of the preceding step cycle. Runners training for shorter races (up to 10-K) can also practice 3-week step cycles, but volume should increase only between the first and second weeks of the step cycle, not from one step cycle to the next. In other words, the volume of training in week 4 of the phase should be the same as in week 1, the volume of training in week 5 should be the same as in week 2, and the volume in recovery week 6 should be the same as in recovery week 3 (as shown in the table "Examples of Weekly Running Volumes [in Miles] in the Build Phase" on page 168). In order to avoid injury and overtraining, all runners need to be very careful when simultaneously increasing the volume of high-intensity training and total running volume. The table shows how a marathoner and a 10-K runner might plan weekly running-volume variations in a 9-week build phase with 3-week step cycles.

In the peak phase, lower-volume runners should gradually increase volume until 1 to 2 weeks before their peak race (unless they race frequently). Higher-volume runners training for longer races (15-K and longer) should continue to gradually increase volume during the first weeks of the peak phase and then sharply decrease volume in the final 2 weeks. Higher-volume runners training for shorter races should maintain a relatively consistent volume that fluctuates in step cycles. All runners need to taper during the final 3 days to 2 weeks before a peak race. As previously mentioned, a taper is a sharp reduction in training volume whose purpose is to allow you to fully absorb the final days of hard training and achieve a state of maximum performance readiness. The

EXAMPLES OF WEEKLY RUNNING VOLUMES (IN MILES) IN THE BUILD PHASE

WEEK	10-K RUNNER	MARATHON RUNNER
11	40	50
12	45	55
13 (Recovery)	35	45
14	40	52
15	45	58
16 (Recovery)	35	45
17	40	54
18	45	60
19 (Recovery)	35	45

longer your peak race and the higher your training volume, the longer your taper should be.

Planning weekly cross-training volume does not require as much thought. Nevertheless, it is important to plan it, because it all requires time and energy that you need to be prepared to use up. One of the main reasons runners fail to cross-train as much as they should is that they plan only their running and just try to "fit in" cross-training. This is the training equivalent of making a lunch date by simply saying, "Let's have lunch sometime soon"—a hollow intention. When we truly intend to do something, we get specific!

Unless you wish to compete in other types of races besides running events, you can plan to do a consistent amount of cross-training throughout the training cycle. You need to stretch and strength-train every week in order to maintain the benefits of these activities, yet because you are not trying to achieve "peak" strength or flexibility, it's fine to do just a small amount every week. You should also plan to do roughly the same amount of endurance cross-training from week to week, with these workouts serving as active recovery.

For the cross-training minimalist, the weekly regimen will most likely entail one active-recovery workout, two strength workouts, and three or four stretching sessions. Runners with special needs or circumstances may do substantially more cross-training in one or more of these modalities. For example, a runner in training for a challenging marathon time goal who cannot handle high running mileage might choose to perform three or more endurance cross-training workouts for aerobic maintenance and active recovery every week.

If you have not been cross-training before the start of the training cycle, you may choose to ease into it, adding one cross-training workout a week until you achieve a full schedule. Plan to do less strength training in the week before any important race—in particular, remove lower-extremity exercises from your strength workouts.

Once you've planned your cross-training schedule, you can finally determine your total number of weekly training hours: Multiply the number of running miles you plan to do that week by your average mile pace, and add to this figure the total amount of time you plan to spend cross-training. Do this for each week of the training cycle. Make sure the totals are realistic.

STEP FOUR: SELECT KEY WORKOUTS

Key workouts are the more challenging runs you perform to stimulate new fitness adaptations. There are many types of key workouts, and each type may be performed at a variety of durations. The number, type, and duration of the key workouts you do will depend on your experience and initial fitness levels, your individual responses to training, and your racing goals. Different types of key workouts are appropriate at different points in the training cycle; in fact, it's the key workouts that really define each phase of training.

Three key workouts per week are sufficient for most runners. Experienced, competitive runners may benefit from doing a fourth key workout most weeks. In recovery weeks, every runner needs to do fewer or shorter key workouts.

A weekly long run should be a key workout for all runners throughout most of the training cycle, because consistent longer runs are essential for increasing endurance and fat metabolism. Naturally, the definition of *long* is relative: Less fit and experienced runners and those training for shorter races will do shorter "long" runs than fitter, more experienced runners and those training for longer races. Whatever your fitness level and peak race, start doing long runs no later than the middle of the base phase, and continue to do them at least 2 out of every 3 weeks until you taper for your peak race.

In the base phase, two foundation runs, each followed by a set of strides, will count as second and third weekly key workouts. Beginning in the middle of the base phase, you may do a fartlek run instead of one of these or as a fourth key workout. A fartlek is a 40-to-60-minute run that's mostly at moderate aerobic intensity but punctuated by six to ten 30-second bursts at speed intensity. Competitive runners training for shorter—and therefore faster—races may do three sets of strides per week, or two sets of strides plus a fartlek run, for a total of four key workouts (including the long run).

In the build phase, you will add some high-intensity key workouts. I recommend beginning this phase with an emphasis on speed-intensity training and then, at about the midpoint of the phase, changing the emphasis to training at aerobic capacity. This is because aerobic-capacity workouts are both more challenging and more race-specific than speed workouts.

Most runners should start the build phase with just one high-intensity workout in the first week to avoid increasing the training workload too abruptly. Starting in the second week of the phase, perform two high-intensity workouts and a long run each week, except when rest is needed or when a short race substitutes for one of the high-intensity runs. When training for longer races, do weekly anaerobic-threshold (AT) workouts in addition to the speed workouts of the first half of the phase and the aerobic-capacity (AC) workouts of the latter half. Those training for shorter races may follow the same pattern but are encouraged to also do one set of strides following a recovery run each week in the second half of the phase to maintain their adaptations to speed training. (This should not be counted as a key workout.) Throughout the phase, each week's third key workout should continue to be a long run.

Inexperienced runners and others who cannot handle much high-intensity running should do just one weekly high-intensity workout: a speed workout throughout the first half of the build phase and an AC workout through the second half. Instead of a second high-intensity workout, do just a set of strides after a recovery or foundation run.

Runners with an extensive training background and a high level of fitness can benefit from doing four key workouts during the build phase, except in recovery weeks. If you're such a runner in training for a shorter peak race, you'll probably want to do three high-intensity workouts—a speed workout, an AC workout, and an AT workout—and one long run. In recovery weeks and race weeks, eliminate one of the three high-intensity runs. If you've never done three high-intensity workouts a week before and you feel ready to try this, approach it as an experiment: Ease into the phase by doing just a speed workout the first week, a speed workout and an AT workout the second week, and all three types of high-intensity workout the next week. Don't be surprised if it's just too much for you. When training for a longer race, do two high-intensity workouts (an AC run and an AT run) and two long runs. The second long run need not be quite as long as the first, but it should be substantially longer than the typical foundation run.

In the peak phase, runners on a schedule of three weekly key workouts who are training for short and long races alike should do a long run, an AT run, and a workout mixing speed and AC work, unless they prefer to do just one high-intensity workout a week, in which case a set of strides can take the place of the mixed-intensity workout. Those training for longer races should perform longer long runs and maintain higher overall training volume than those training for shorter races. If your peak race is a marathon, do two or three marathon-pace workouts, spaced every other week or so, in place of two or three long runs.

If you prefer four key workouts and are training for shorter races, your four key workouts should be a long run, an AT run, a workout mixing speed and AC effort, and either a race or a second AT run (ideally in a different format—cruise intervals instead of a tempo run, for example). In recovery weeks, only three key workouts should be completed. If you prefer four key workouts and are training for longer races, do two long runs, an AT run, and a workout mixing speed and AC efforts each week except recovery weeks, when either the second long run or the mixed-intensity workout can be skipped. Be sure that two or three of your long runs are marathon-pace workouts, too.

There are many ways to do each type of key workout. Long runs, including marathon-pace runs, are variable in duration, while the three types of high-intensity workout vary by the number and duration of intervals and sometimes by the duration of active recoveries. In all three phases of the training cycle, the formats you choose need to be appropriate to your fitness level and progressive—that is, they should be

KEY WORKOUTS

	BASE PHASE, 1ST HALF	BASE PHASE, 2ND HALF	BUILD PHASE, 1ST HALF	BUILD PHASE, 2ND HALF	PEAK PHASE
Shorter Peak Race, 3 Key Workouts	1. Long run 2. Strides 3. Strides	1. Long run 2. Strides 3. Strides or fartlek	1. Speed run 2. Long run 3. AT run or strides	1. AC run 2. Long run 3. AT run or strides	1. AT run 2. Mix run or strides 3. Long run
Shorter Peak Race, 4 Key Workouts	1. Long run 2. Strides 3. Strides 4. Strides	1. Long run 2. Strides or fartlek 3. Strides 4. Strides	1. Speed run 2. AC run 3. Long run 4. AT run	1. AC run 2. Speed run 3. Long run 4. AT run	1. AT run 2. Mix run 3. Long run 4. AT run or race
Longer Peak Race, 3 Key Workouts	1. Long run 2. Strides 3. Strides	1. Long run 2. Strides 3. Strides or fartlek	1. Speed run 2. Long run 3. AT run	1. AC run 2. Long run 3. AT run	1. AT run 2. Long run or MP run 3. Mix run
Longer Peak Race, 4 Key Workouts	1. Long run 2. Strides 3. Strides 4. Strides	1. Long run 2. Fartlek 3. Strides 4. Strides	1. Speed run 2. Long run 3. AT run 4. Long run	1. AC run 2. Long run 3. AT run 4. Long run	1. AT run 2. Long run or MP run 3. Long run 4. Mix run

AC run = aerobic-capacity run (lactate intervals)
AT run = anaerobic-threshold run
Mix run = mix of AC and speed efforts
MP run = marathon-pace run
Strides = endurance run followed by 4–6 strides

performed for a longer duration or at a faster pace each time they are repeated, more or less.

The table on the opposite page summarizes the suggested key workouts for various categories of runner in each of the three training phases. Workouts are listed in descending order of importance. This means that the number one run in each list should be your highest priority of each week, your most challenging workout of the week, and the workout for which you are best rested. In recovery weeks, race weeks, taper weeks, and the initial weeks of the build phase, you may choose to forgo one or two of the lower-priority key workouts.

Once you have determined the number and formats of your key workouts, go ahead and schedule them in your training calendar. The guiding principle is to schedule them in such a way that you are fairly well-recovered from each when it comes time to do the next, which generally entails spreading them out during the week as much as possible. If you do four key workouts each week, you'll have to do at least one pair of them on consecutive days. Some runners are able to do back-to-back high-intensity workouts. I do better when I follow a high-intensity workout with a long run. You may need to experiment.

STEP FIVE: SCHEDULE FOUNDATION RUNS AND ACTIVE RECOVERIES

Your training schedule now contains all of your planned races and key workouts, plus your target running and total training volumes. Now all you need to do to complete your plan is to schedule your foundation runs and your active recoveries, the latter of which can be either easy runs or cross-training. Determine how much additional training you need to do to meet your weekly running and total training volumes, decide which modality you want to use for your active recoveries, and choose the mornings or afternoons on which you would like to perform each workout. Little or no detail is required. Simply fill in your calendar by dropping in phrases like "easy run" or "strength workout." In fact, to build some flexibility into your schedule, you may even drop in the word "easy" and decide only when the time arrives whether to do a foundation run, an active-recovery run, active-recovery cross-training, or nothing.

MAKING ADJUSTMENTS

Too often, runners become slaves to their training programs. "It says here I'm supposed to do a dozen 400m intervals on the track this afternoon. So what if I planned this workout 6 months ago and I'm so sore and exhausted from yesterday's training that I can barely climb a flight of stairs? A plan is a plan!"

Understand that to truly benefit from your key workouts, you must be physically ready to perform them at or near the limit of your current ability. Since you cannot know whether you're ready for a hard workout until it's actually time to do it, you should view all key workouts as tentatively scheduled. By all means, do your best to plan well so that you seldom come to a key workout unready. But whenever you do feel flat before or at the beginning of a key workout, immediately pull the ripcord and either take the day off or perform an active-recovery workout instead. You can always push back the key workout a day or two or scrap it altogether.

By the same token, when you begin a scheduled recovery workout feeling especially good, you may choose to take advantage of your readiness and instead perform a more demanding workout that you had scheduled for later in the week. The whole idea is to do your key workouts when your body is most ready for them, which requires some spontaneity. Don't get me wrong—a training plan is indispensable. Treating it as gospel, though, is an all-too-common mistake.

Learning to better gauge your recovery status by objective and subjective means will help you become more adept at determining what type of training you need on any given day. I recommend that, first thing each morning, you take your pulse, weigh yourself, and do a few deep squats to gauge muscle soreness, strength, and energy. Enter the results in your training log along with the particulars of any workouts you perform that day. After a while, you will begin to notice patterns. Generally, when your pulse is up, your weight is down, or your deep squats go poorly, you will feel worse in your workouts. Once you've identified these patterns, you can tweak your workout plans each morning to ensure that you train hard when you're well-recovered and take it easy when you're not.

Your weekly training-volume goals should always be subject to adjustment as well. While it is beneficial to set a goal to perform a quantified amount of training in a week, do not treat this total as an absolute must. If, in a given week, 27 miles of running turns out to be the right amount for you, squeezing out an additional 3 miles just to hit a volume goal of 30 will essentially undo part of what you achieved with the first 27. Again, let your body tell you how much is enough.

Even the 7-day weekly cycle should be viewed as optional. It is perfectly within the realm of possibility that, say, two high-intensity runs within a 7-day span is too much for you, while two in a 10-day period is just right. Let your body, rather than convention, guide you. (You may recall my having mentioned in a previous chapter that Paula Radcliffe uses an 8-day "week.") Weekly cycles are definitely the place to begin: They're convenient and they do work for many runners. Still, be ready to do certain types of key workout less often if repeating them every 7 days wears you down.

Injury, illness, or protracted distractions in other domains of your life can cause unplanned lapses in training that necessitate major adjustments. The specific nature of these adjustments depends on many factors, including the nature of the injury, illness, or stressor; its duration; the point at which it falls in the training cycle; and so forth. Generally, when you miss a week or so of training and come back with a sound body, you'll find no significant adjustment necessary. If you miss a couple of weeks and come back sound, you'll probablyw ant to give yourself slightly toned-down workouts for another full week.

Longer lapses may require an adjustment in your race plans. At the very least, you will probably need to replan the remaining weeks of your training cycle in such a way that it carries you from your *current* level of fitness to the highest fitness peak you can manage in the time available. Don't make any decisions one way or the other, though, until after you've resumed semi-normal training for a week or 10 days and assessed how much fitness you've lost.

REFINING NEVER ENDS

Regardless of how healthy you remain, how fit you become, and how well you race in any given training cycle, your next training cycle should never be quite the same. There should always be at least one specific way in which the next plan represents a refinement of the previous.

MEB KEFLEZIGHI

Cross-training is one of the best improvisational tools that runners can use to keep their training on track when unexpected setbacks arise. A terrific example of this use of cross-training comes from Mebrahtom "Meb" Keflezighi's preparations for the 2004 U.S. Olympic Trials Marathon. The American record holder at 10,000 meters, Keflezighi was a strong favorite to earn one of three slots on the U.S. team that would compete in Sydney. But in the middle of his ramp-up, he caught a flu that lasted for 3 weeks and caused him to miss a lot of scheduled running. Consequently, in order to avoid injuring himself, he had to limit the amount of running he did even when he finally felt healthy enough to run regularly again.

Keflezighi had already used endurance cross-training earlier in the training period to train through a case of knee tendinitis. Now, as he fought off the flu and worked his way back into full training, he combined runs with long bike rides (1.5 to 2 hours) and frequent high-intensity pool runs to build his fitness without subjecting his legs to the level of impact forces they would endure if every workout were a land run.

With his coach, Bob Larsen, Keflezighi figured out the minimum amount of quality running he would need to be able to do in the time remaining to avoid scratching from the trials. He did scratch from a planned tune-up race. Thanks to this careful approach, Keflezighi was able to complete 3 solid weeks of peak training before it was time to taper and finished second at the trials in 2:11:47, just 5 seconds behind winner Alan Culpepper.

Those familiar axioms "Don't mess with success" and "If it ain't broke, don't fix it" don't apply in running. The reason is that every successful training plan *changes* you for the better. If your training was truly optimal in your most recent training cycle, you will be capable of a higher level of training in the next, and it would be foolish not to take advantage of this opportunity. Your challenge during the transition phase is to figure out just how to take advantage of it.

Should you try a little more mileage? A slightly less minimalist approach to cross-training? More high-intensity running? Deciding exactly what to try will not be difficult if you always pay close attention to how your body and mind respond to training as you go. Keeping a detailed training log helps as well. The combination of subjective self-analysis and a solid record of the facts of your training will give you some specific ideas.

For example, in reflecting on your most recent training, you might realize that while you were generally pleased with the way your endurance and speed came around, you consistently wished for more power when running at higher speeds and up hills. Looking over your training logs, you see that you did very little training to improve your power. So you resolve to do more power-strength-training workouts going forward, as well as more drills such as high knees and butt kicks, plus some harder hill running.

Or you might decide to do something else entirely. Just do *something* different!

SEVEN

SAMPLE TRAINING PROGRAMS

THIS CHAPTER PRESENTS five complete sample training programs: a basic 10-K program, an advanced 10-K/half-marathon program, a basic marathon program, an advanced marathon program, and a runner's triathlon program. I offer these not with an expectation that you will follow any one of them to the letter but with the hope that you will be able to use one or more of them as templates that you can further customize to fit your precise situation. Approach them with a creative mindset, as a prodigal young jazz singer approaches an old swing standard.

Each program has built-in flexibility in terms of the duration of each workout, weekly training volume, and the types and number of cross-training workouts you perform. Tailor these aspects of the program as appropriate. Most of the other tweaks you may need to make will have to do with which workouts you perform on which days. For example, all of the programs assume a normal Saturday/Sunday weekend and accordingly bunch training into this 2-day period. But suppose Tuesdays and Fridays are your days off from work—and therefore your best opportunities for training. You'll have to tweak.

In three of the following five programs, it's also unlikely that you will always want or be able to schedule prepeak races to coincide with the ones plotted. So you'll probably need to adjust your schedule accordingly.

The key workouts are indicated by a dark gray shaded background (except in the triathlon program, in which almost every workout is a key workout, in a sense). These are the least dispensable parts of the program, and they're the least likely to be improved through creative customization. The type, frequency, and order of the key workouts should remain more or less as presented, because I have fixed these parameters on the basis of what appears to work best for all runners of a given training level preparing for a given type of event. So I urge you to try to do every key workout as described. You should, however, feel free to move these workouts around within the week so that you consistently do them when you are most ready for them.

In the left column of each program, both the program week number and the phase week number are given, except for the basic 10-K program (because of its brevity). If a given week is intended to be a recovery week, this fact is also noted in the left column.

All workouts are described in detail in the text that follows the schedules. Finally, note that there are no formally scheduled stretching sessions in the programs. Be sure to stretch at least three times a week and preferably daily. Stretching after runs and endurance cross-training workouts is especially beneficial. Stretching between strength exercises in your strength workouts is another convenient option. Again, I recommend stretching or performing range-of-motion drills after the warmup that precedes all high-intensity runs.

BASIC 10-K PROGRAM

This program is appropriate for new runners, those who are returning to training after a long layoff, and casual runners who want to train consistently but not too hard. It is 12 weeks long and culminates in a 10-K race, the only scheduled race in the program. It represents a single phase combining elements of base and peak training.

BASIC 10-K PROGRAM

	DAY 1	DAY 2	DAY 3	DAY 4	DAY 5	DAY 6	DAY 7
Week 1	Off	Easy run	Easy X	Strength	Easy run	Easy X Strength	Easy run
Week 2	Off	Easy run	Easy X	Strength	Easy run	Easy X Strength	Easy run
Week 3	Off	Easy run	Easy X	Strength	Easy run	Easy X Strength	Endurance run
Week 4	Off	Easy run	Easy X	Strength	Easy run	Easy X Strength	Endurance run
Week 5	Off	Easy run + strides	Easy X	Strength	Easy run + strides	Easy X Strength	Endurance run
Week 6	Off	Easy run + strides	Easy X	Strength	Easy run + strides	Easy X Strength	Endurance run
Week 7	Off	Easy run + strides	Easy X	Strength	AT run	Easy X Strength	Endurance run
Week 8	Off	Easy run + strides	Easy X	Strength	AT run	Easy X Strength	Endurance run
Week 9	Off	Fartlek	Easy X	Strength	AT run	Easy X Strength	Time trial
Week 10	Off	Fartlek	Easy X	Strength	AT run	Easy X Strength	Long run
Week 11	Off	Fartlek	Easy X	Strength	AT run	Easy X Strength	Endurance run
Week 12	Off	Fartlek	Easy X	Strength	Easy run	Off	**10-K race**

WORKOUT DESCRIPTIONS

EASY RUN: Perform a steady recovery- or moderate-aerobic-intensity (foundation) run of 20 to 40 minutes, depending on what your body is ready for.

EASY RUN + STRIDES: Perform an easy run as described above, and follow it with a set of strides: four to six speed-intensity runs of about 100 yards each, separated by recovery jogs.

EASY X: Perform a steady-pace endurance cross-training workout of 30 to 60 minutes, depending on what your body is ready for.

STRENGTH: Perform a 20-minute strengthening workout using the guidelines provided in chapter 2. You may wish to mix strengthening exercises with flexibility exercises.

ENDURANCE RUN: Perform a steady-pace moderate- to high-aerobic-intensity run lasting 40 to 60 minutes.

AT RUN: Between a warmup and cooldown at recovery intensity, run for 16 to 24 minutes (16 minutes in your first AT run, working your way up to 24 minutes in the last) at anaerobic-threshold intensity.

FARTLEK: Run 40 to 60 minutes, mostly at moderate-aerobic intensity, but toss in six to ten 30-second bursts at speed intensity.

TIME TRIAL: Between a warmup and a cooldown, run 10 kilometers (or 6 miles, if it's more convenient) on a measured course at a 95 to 99 percent effort level. This workout will prepare your mind and body for the coming actual race experience and will give you a goal time to shoot for.

LONG RUN: Perform a steady-pace moderate- to high-aerobic-intensity run lasting 60 to 80 minutes.

ADVANCED 10-K/HALF-MARATHON PROGRAM

This is a 24-week training program for runners seeking a maximum performance at distances ranging from 10-K to the half-marathon. It calls for cardiovascular workouts 7 days a week except in recovery weeks. Three or four of these are also key workouts.

Three days a week, in most weeks, you have the option to perform an easy run, an easy endurance cross-training workout, or both. After an initial ramp-up in the first few weeks, you should try to perform a consistent total number of workouts each week. In other words, if you want to double on these option days, try to do so consistently every week; whereas if you prefer to avoid doubling, be sure to consistently perform either a run or an endurance cross-training workout on these option days. In any case, do at least one of these workouts in a nonimpact endurance cross-training discipline each week.

Five races are scheduled: a 5-K in week 11, a 10-K in each of weeks 14 and 17, and your choice of a 10-K or half-marathon in weeks 20 and 24. Naturally, chances are slim that your own racing schedule will work out to match this template, but I do recommend trying to race about this often, at these times, and at these distances. Your first two or three races will serve mainly to increase your fitness. The last two or three will be the real performance opportunities.

ADVANCED 10-K/HALF-MARATHON PROGRAM

	DAY 1	DAY 2	DAY 3	DAY 4	DAY 5	DAY 6	DAY 7
Week 1 Base 1	Easy X	Easy run	Easy run or easy X Strength	Easy run	Easy run and/or easy X	Easy run or easy X Strength	Long run
Week 2 Base 2	Off	Easy run	Easy run and/or easy X Strength	Easy run	Easy run and/or easy X	Easy run or easy X Strength	Long run
Week 3 Base 3	Easy X	Easy run	Easy run and/or easy X Strength	Easy run	Easy run and/or easy X	Easy run and/or easy X Strength	Long run
Week 4 Base 4 Recovery	Off	Easy run + strides	Easy run and/or easy X Strength	Fartlek	Easy run and/or easy X	Easy run and/or easy X Strength	Long run
Week 5 Base 5	Easy X	Easy run + strides	Easy run and/or easy X Strength	Fartlek	Easy run and/or easy X	Easy run and/or easy X Strength	Long run

(continued)

ADVANCED 10-K/HALF-MARATHON PROGRAM (*cont.*)

	DAY 1	DAY 2	DAY 3	DAY 4	DAY 5	DAY 6	DAY 7
Week 6 Base 6	Easy X	Easy run + strides	Easy run and/or easy X Strength	Fartlek	Easy run and/or easy X	Easy run and/or easy X Strength	Long run
Week 7 Build 1	Easy X	AT run	Easy run and/or easy X Strength	Fartlek	Easy run and/or easy X	Easy run and/or easy X Strength	Long run
Week 8 Build 2 Recovery	Off	AT run	Easy run and/or easy X Strength	Fartlek	Easy run and/or easy X	Easy run and/or easy X Strength	Long run
Week 9 Build 3	Easy X	AT run	Easy run and/or easy X Strength	SI run	Easy run and/or easy X	Easy run and/or easy X Strength	Long run
Week 10 Build 4	Easy X	AT run	Easy run and/or easy X Strength	SI run	Easy run and/or easy X	Endurance run or X + optional easy X or run Strength	Long run
Week 11 Build 5 Recovery	Off	AT run	Easy run and/or easy X Strength	SI run	Easy run and/or easy X	Easy run and/or easy X Strength	5-K race
Week 12 Build 6	Easy X	AT run	Easy run and/or easy X Strength	SI run	Easy run and/or easy X	Endurance run or X + optional easy X or run Strength	Long run
Week 13 Build 7	Easy X	AT run	Easy run and/or easy X Strength	LI run	Easy run and/or easy X	Endurance run or X + optional easy X or run Strength	Long run

	DAY 1	DAY 2	DAY 3	DAY 4	DAY 5	DAY 6	DAY 7
Week 14 Build 8 Recovery	Off	AT run	Easy run and/or easy X Strength	Easy run	Easy run and/or easy X	Easy run and/or easy X	10-K race
Week 15 Build 9	Easy X	AT run	Easy run and/or easy X Strength	LI run	Easy run and/or easy X	Endurance run or X + optional easy X or run Strength	Long run
Week 16 Build 10	Easy X	MP run (10)	Easy run and/or easy X Strength	LI run	Easy run and/or easy X	Endurance run or X + optional easy X or run Strength	Long run
Week 17 Peak 1 Recovery	Off	AT run	Easy run and/or easy X Strength	Easy run	Easy run and/or easy X	Easy run and/or easy X	10-K race
Week 18 Peak 2	Easy X	AT run	Easy run and/or easy X Strength	LI run	Easy run and/or easy X	Easy run and/or easy X Strength	Long run
Week 19 Peak 3	Easy X	MP run (12)	Easy run and/or easy X Strength	MI run	Easy run and/or easy X	Endurance run or X + optional easy X or run Strength	Long run
Week 20 Peak 4 Recovery	Off	Easy run	Easy run and/or easy X Strength	MI run	Easy run + strides	Easy run or easy X	10-K race or half-marathon

(*continued*)

ADVANCED 10-K/HALF-MARATHON PROGRAM (*cont.*)

	DAY 1	DAY 2	DAY 3	DAY 4	DAY 5	DAY 6	DAY 7
Week 21 Peak 5	Easy X	AT run	Easy run and/or easy X Strength	MI run	Easy run and/or easy X	Endurance run or X + optional easy X or run Strength	Long run
Week 22 Peak 6	Easy X	AT run	Easy run and/or easy X Strength	MI run	Easy run and/or easy X	Easy run and/or easy X Strength	Long run
Week 23 Peak 7	Off	AT run	Easy run Strength	MI run	Easy run or easy X	Easy run or easy X	Endurance run
Week 24 Peak 8 Recovery	Off	Easy run	Easy run or easy X	Easy run	Race prep	Off	10-K race or half-marathon

WORKOUT DESCRIPTIONS

EASY RUN: Perform a steady recovery- or moderate-aerobic-intensity (foundation) run of 30 to 60 minutes, depending on what your body is ready for.

EASY X: Perform a steady recovery- or moderate-aerobic-intensity endurance cross-training workout of 30 to 60 minutes, depending on what your body is ready for.

EASY RUN OR EASY X: Do either of the two workouts just described.

EASY RUN AND/OR EASY X: Perform an easy (recovery or foundation) run, an easy endurance cross-training workout, or both (with at least 4 hours of separation). Each (or either) workout should last 30 to 60 minutes, depending on what your body is ready for.

STRENGTH: Perform a 20-minute strengthening workout using the guidelines provided in chapter 2. You may wish to mix strengthening exercises with flexibility exercises.

LONG RUN: Do a moderate- to high-aerobic-intensity run that lasts long enough to leave you moderately fatigued at the end. Your first one should be about 10 percent longer than the longest easy run

Many runners who have branched out to the sport of triathlon have found that multisport training, far from impeding their running, has actually made them better runners. Canadian Carol Montgomery is a noteworthy example.

Montgomery ran track and cross-country in secondary school and competed in road races throughout her college years. After completing college, she took up triathlon and excelled immediately, earning her first Canadian National Triathlon Team selection and a World Championship silver medal in 1989. Over the next few years, her running improved so much that she began competing on Canadian national running teams as well. In 1993, she represented her country in the World Cross-Country Championships. Two years later, she won a silver medal in the 5000m and a bronze in the 10,000m at the PanAm Games.

In 2000, Montgomery made history by qualifying for the Canadian Olympic team in triathlon and in the 10,000m run (with a qualifying time of 32:11). Other runners were amazed that Montgomery was able to do the latter despite running just 35 to 40 miles a week, but Montgomery felt that the 8 weekly hours of cycling she did more than made up the difference without increasing her chances of getting injured.

you have done recently. Gradually increase the duration of your long runs throughout the program until they reach an appropriate maximum duration, after which they can level off (assuming the maximum is reached before your final recovery week). You should reach at least 18 miles but need not exceed 22 miles. Shorten your long run in recovery weeks by 10 to 20 percent as compared to the previous week.

EASY RUN + STRIDES: Perform an easy (foundation) run as described earlier, followed by a set of strides: four to six speed-intensity runs of about 100 yards each, separated by recovery jogs.

FARTLEK: Run for 40 to 60 minutes, mostly at moderate aerobic intensity, but toss in six to ten 30-second bursts at speed intensity.

AT RUN: Between a warmup and a cooldown at recovery intensity, do 12 to 40 minutes of anaerobic-threshold running, but not more than 20 minutes consecutively. When breaking up your AT work into intervals, jog for at least 4 minutes between them. Increase the duration of the workout each time you repeat it. For example, your first AT run might be broken into two 10-minute intervals (2 × 10 minutes), with your last one topping out at 2 × 20 minutes. Your pace will also gradually increase as you gain fitness. Shorten your recovery-week AT runs unless you feel great.

SI RUN: Between a warmup and a cooldown, do 8 to 12 intervals of 400m or 4 to 10 intervals of 400m plus 4 intervals of 200m, all at speed intensity. Jog 400m after each hard effort. Start with a workout duration that you can handle, and increase it as necessary over the ensuing weeks. Shorten your recovery-week SI run in week 11 unless you feel great.

ENDURANCE RUN OR X + OPTIONAL EASY X OR RUN: Perform a moderate- to high-aerobic-intensity run or endurance cross-training workout that lasts at least 1 hour. If you wish, also do a shorter recovery-intensity workout (a run if you cross-trained earlier or cross-training if you ran earlier), with at least 4 hours between the two workouts.

LI RUN: Run four to seven lactate intervals lasting 4 to 5 minutes each at aerobic-capacity intensity, with 3 to 4 minutes of active recovery between intervals. Start with a workout duration that you can handle, and increase it as necessary over the ensuing weeks.

MP RUN: Following a warmup, run the number of miles given between parentheses at your marathon pace.

MI RUN: Do a mixed-intervals run with speed intervals of 200 to 400 meters and lactate intervals lasting 4 to 5 minutes, with appropriate recoveries. A shorter workout might be 2 × 400m, 2 × 1200m, 2 × 200m. A longer one might be 3 × 400, 3 × 1200, 3 × 400. Start with a workout duration that you can handle, and increase it as necessary over the ensuing weeks.

RACE PREP: In the morning, between a brief warmup and cooldown, complete a near-maximum effort lasting 150 seconds, recover for 3 minutes, and then sprint for 30 seconds. You may run, pool run, or ride a bike. Immediately after finishing this workout, consume 12 to 16 ounces of a sports or recovery drink. Maintain a carbohydrate-rich diet for the remainder of the day. This regimen will maximize glycogen storage in your liver and legs for the coming race.

BASIC MARATHON PROGRAM

This is an 18-week program for first-time marathoners and any other runners who would like to try a low-mileage approach to training for a successful marathon. In this program, you will never run more than 4 days a week, and you will perform two endurance cross-training workouts weekly. There is one prepeak race, a 10-K, scheduled at the end of week 13.

BASIC MARATHON PROGRAM

	DAY 1	DAY 2	DAY 3	DAY 4	DAY 5	DAY 6	DAY 7
Week 1 Base 1	Off	Easy run	Easy X Strength	Off	Easy run Strength	Easy X	Long run (4)
Week 2 Base 2	Off	Easy run	Easy X Strength	Off	Easy run Strength	Easy X	Long run (5)
Week 3 Base 3	Off	Easy run + strides or fartlek	Easy X Strength	Easy run + strides or fartlek	Easy X Strength	Easy run	Long run (6)
Week 4 Base 4 Recovery	Off	Easy run + strides or fartlek	Easy X Strength	Off	Easy run Strength	Easy X	Long run (0)
Week 5 Base 5	Off	Easy run + strides or fartlek	Easy X Strength	Easy run + strides or fartlek	Easy X Strength	Easy run	Long run (10)
Week 6 Base 6	Off	Easy run + strides or fartlek	Easy X Strength	Easy run + strides or fartlek	Easy X Strength	Easy run	Long run (12)
Week 7 Build 1 Recovery	Off	Easy run + drills	Easy X Strength	SI run	Easy X Strength	Easy run or off	Long run (10)
Week 8 Build 2	Off	Easy run + drills	Easy X Strength	SI run	Easy X Strength	Easy run	Long run (14)
Week 9 Build 3	Off	Easy run + drills	Easy X Strength	SI run	Easy X Strength	Easy run	Long run (16)

(continued)

	DAY 1	DAY 2	DAY 3	DAY 4	DAY 5	DAY 6	DAY 7

BASIC MARATHON PROGRAM (*cont.*)

	DAY 1	DAY 2	DAY 3	DAY 4	DAY 5	DAY 6	DAY 7
Week 10 Build 4 Recovery	Off	Easy run + drills	Easy X Strength	SI run	Strength	Easy run	Long run (12)
Week 11 Build 5	Off	Easy run + strides or fartlek	Easy X Strength	LI run	Easy X Strength	Easy run or off	Long run (18)
Week 12 Build 6	Off	Easy run + strides or fartlek	Easy X Strength	LI run	Easy X Strength	Easy run	Long run (20)
Week 13 Build 7	Off	Easy run + strides or fartlek	Easy X Strength	LI run	Easy X Strength	Off	10-K race
Week 14 Build 8	Off	Easy run + strides or fartlek	Easy X Strength	LI run	Easy X Strength	Easy run	Long run (20)
Week 15 Peak 1	Off	Easy run + strides or fartlek	Easy X Strength	AT run	Easy X Strength	Easy run	Long run (22)
Week 16 Peak 2	Off	Easy run + strides or fartlek	Easy X Strength	AT run	Easy X Strength	Easy run	Long run (15)
Week 17 Peak 3 Recovery	Off	Easy run + strides or fartlek	Easy X Strength	AT run	Easy X Strength	Easy run or off	Long run (12)
Week 18 Peak 4 Recovery	Off	Easy run + strides or fartlek	Easy X	AT run	Race prep	Off	**Marathon**

Workout Descriptions

EASY RUN: Perform a steady recovery- or moderate-aerobic-intensity (foundation) run of 30 to 60 minutes, depending on what your body is ready for.

EASY RUN + STRIDES OR FARTLEK: Perform an easy run as described above, either followed by strides (four to six 100-yard speed runs separated by recovery jogs) or in the form of a fartlek, in which the easy pace is interrupted by six to ten 30-second bursts at speed intensity.

EASY RUN + DRILLS: Do an easy run as described earlier, followed by one set of each of the four strength-building running drills described at the end of chapter 2.

EASY X: Perform a steady recovery- or moderate-aerobic-intensity endurance cross-training workout of 30 to 60 minutes, depending on what your body is ready for.

STRENGTH: Perform a 20-minute strengthening workout using the guidelines provided in chapter 2. You may wish to mix strengthening exercises with flexibility exercises.

LONG RUN: Run approximately the specified distance at a steady low-to-moderate pace.

SI RUN: Between a warmup and a cooldown, run six to eight intervals of 400m at speed intensity. Jog 400m after each hard effort. Do six intervals in your first SI run, and add intervals as necessary in subsequent SI runs.

LI RUN: Run four to six lactate intervals lasting 4 minutes each at aerobic-capacity intensity, with 3 to 4 minutes of active recovery between intervals. Do four intervals in your first LI run, and add intervals in subsequent LI runs if you feel able.

AT RUN: Between a warmup and a cooldown at recovery intensity, run for 20 minutes at anaerobic-threshold intensity. Your pace will gradually increase during the course of the program.

RACE PREP: In the morning, between a brief warmup and cooldown, complete a near-maximum effort lasting 150 seconds, recover for 3 minutes, and then sprint for 30 seconds. You may run, pool run, or ride a bike. Immediately after finishing this workout, consume 12 to 16 ounces of a sports or recovery drink. Maintain a carbohydrate-rich diet for the remainder of the day. This regimen will maximize glycogen storage in your liver and legs for the coming race.

ADVANCED MARATHON PROGRAM

This is a 24-week training program for experienced runners who are willing and able to train hard to achieve a peak performance at the marathon distance. It calls for cardiovascular workouts, including three or four key workouts, 7 days a week except in recovery weeks.

For 3 days out of most weeks, you have the option of performing an easy run, an easy endurance cross-training workout, or both. After an initial ramp-up in the first few weeks, you should try to perform a consistent total number of workouts each week. So if you want to double on these option days, try to do so every week. If you prefer to avoid doubling, be sure to consistently perform either a run or an endurance cross-training workout on these option days. In any case, make at least one of these workouts a nonimpact endurance cross-training workout each week.

Three tune-up races are scheduled within the program: a 5-K in week 14, a 10-K in week 17, and a half-marathon in week 20. I think that racing this much, at these distances, and at these times while training for a peak marathon is ideal, but it is not the only way.

ADVANCED MARATHON PROGRAM							
	DAY 1	DAY 2	DAY 3	DAY 4	DAY 5	DAY 6	DAY 7
Week 1 Base 1	Easy X	Easy run	Easy run or easy X Strength	Easy run	Easy run and/or easy X	Easy run or easy X Strength	Long run (8)
Week 2 Base 2	Off	Easy run	Easy run and/or easy X Strength	Easy run	Easy run and/or easy X	Easy run or easy X Strength	Long run (9)
Week 3 Base 3	Easy X	Easy run	Easy run and/or easy X Strength	Easy run	Easy run and/or easy X	Easy run and/or easy X Strength	Long run (10)

ADVANCED MARATHON PROGRAM (*cont.*)

	DAY 1	DAY 2	DAY 3	DAY 4	DAY 5	DAY 6	DAY 7
Week 4 **Base 4** **Recovery**	Off	Easy run + strides or fartlek	Easy run and/or easy X Strength	Easy run + strides or fartlek	Easy run and/or easy X	Easy run and/or easy X Strength	Long run (6)
Week 5 **Base 5**	Easy X	Hilly run + strides	Easy run and/or easy X Strength	Easy run + strides or fartlek	Easy run and/or easy X	Easy run and/or easy X Strength	Long run (12)
Week 6 **Base 6**	Easy X	Hilly run + strides	Easy run and/or easy X Strength	Easy run + strides or fartlek	Easy run and/or easy X	Easy run and/or easy X Strength	Long run (13)
Week 7 **Build 1**	Easy X	Hilly run + strides	Easy run and/or easy X Strength	Fartlek	Easy run and/or easy X	Easy run and/or easy X Strength	Long run (14)
Week 8 **Build 2** **Recovery**	Off	Hilly run + strides	Easy run and/or easy X Strength	Fartlek	Easy run and/or easy X	Easy run and/or easy X Strength	Long run (12)
Week 9 **Build 3**	Easy X	AT run	Easy run and/or easy X Strength	SI run	Easy run and/or easy X	Easy run and/or easy X Strength	Long run (15)
Week 10 **Build 4**	Easy X	AT run	Easy run and/or easy X Strength	SI run	Easy run and/or easy X	Endurance run + optional easy X Strength	Long run (16)
Week 11 **Build 5** **Recovery**	Off	AT run	Easy run and/or easy X Strength	SI run	Easy run and/or easy X	Easy run and/or easy X Strength	Long run (14)

(continued)

ADVANCED MARATHON PROGRAM (*cont.*)

	DAY 1	DAY 2	DAY 3	DAY 4	DAY 5	DAY 6	DAY 7
Week 12 Build 6	Easy X	AT run	Easy run and/or easy X Strength	SI run	Easy run and/or easy X	Endurance run + optional easy X Strength	Long run (18)
Week 13 Build 7	Easy X	AT run	Easy run and/or easy X Strength	LI run	Easy run and/or easy X	Endurance run + optional easy X Strength	Long run (18)
Week 14 Build 8 Recovery	Off	AT run	Easy run and/or easy X Strength	Easy run	Easy run and/or easy X	Easy run and/or easy X	5-K race
Week 15 Build 9	Easy X	AT run	Easy run and/or easy X Strength	LI run	Easy run and/or easy X	Endurance run + optional easy X Strength	Long run (20)
Week 16 Build 10	Easy X	MP run (10)	Easy run and/or easy X Strength	LI run	Easy run and/or easy X	Endurance run + optional easy X Strength	Long run (20)
Week 17 Peak 1 Recovery	Off	AT run	Easy run and/or easy X Strength	Easy run	Easy run and/or easy X	Easy run and/or easy X	10-K race
Week 18 Peak 2	Easy X	AT run	Easy run and/or easy X Strength	LI run	Easy run and/or easy X	Easy run and/or easy X Strength	Long run (22)

	DAY 1	DAY 2	DAY 3	DAY 4	DAY 5	DAY 6	DAY 7
Week 19 Peak 3	Easy X	MP run (12)	Easy run and/or easy X Strength	MI run	Easy run and/or easy X	Endurance run + optional easy X Strength	Long run (22)
Week 20 Peak 4 Recovery	Off	Easy run	Easy run and/or easy X Strength	MI run	Race prep	Easy run and/or easy X	Half-marathon
Week 21 Peak 5	Easy X	AT run	Easy run and/or easy X Strength	MI run	Easy run and/or easy X	Endurance run + optional easy X Strength	Long run (24)
Week 22 Peak 6	Easy X	MP run (14)	Easy run and/or easy X Strength	MI run	Easy run and/or easy X	Easy run and/or easy X Strength	Long run (18)
Week 23 Peak 7	Off	AT run	Easy run Strength	MI run	Easy run or easy X	Easy run or easy X	Long run (15)
Week 24 Peak 8 Recovery	Off	Easy run	Easy run or easy X	Easy run or easy X	Race Prep	Easy run or easy X	**Marathon**

WORKOUT DESCRIPTIONS

EASY RUN: Perform a steady recovery- or moderate-aerobic-intensity run of 30 to 60 minutes, depending on what your body is ready for.

EASY RUN + STRIDES OR FARTLEK: Perform an easy run as described above, either followed by strides (four to six 100-yard speed runs separated by recovery jogs) or in the form of a fartlek, in which the easy pace is interrupted by six to ten 30-second bursts at speed intensity.

EASY X: Perform a steady recovery- or moderate-aerobic-intensity endurance cross-training workout of 30 to 60 minutes, depending on what your body is ready for.

EASY RUN OR EASY X: Do either type of workout as described earlier.

STRENGTH: Perform a 20-minute strengthening workout using the guidelines provided in chapter 2. You may wish to mix strengthening exercises with flexibility exercises.

EASY RUN AND/OR EASY X: Perform an easy run, an easy endurance cross-training workout, or both (with at least 4 hours of separation). Each (or either) workout should last 30 to 60 minutes, depending on what your body is ready for.

LONG RUN: Run approximately the specified distance, unless you are unable to do so for whatever reason, in which case you should run until you are well-fatigued but not exhausted. If you have already been doing long runs consistently prior to starting this program, you can run a little longer than the specified distance in the base phase. In weeks 1 through 12, complete these runs at an easy pace (moderate-aerobic). In weeks 13 to 22, make them more challenging (moderate- to high-aerobic). One option is to slightly increase your pace every 3 miles or so. Another option is to run all but the last 5 miles at an easy pace and then run the remainder near marathon-race pace.

HILLY RUN + STRIDES: Run on a hilly route at moderate-to-high aerobic intensity for 40 to 70 minutes and then do a set of six strides.

FARTLEK: Run for 40 to 60 minutes at moderate aerobic intensity with a handful of speed-intensity bursts (20 to 60 seconds each) between chosen landmarks.

AT RUN: Between a warmup and a cooldown at recovery intensity, do between 12 and 40 minutes of anaerobic-threshold running, but not more than 20 minutes consecutively. When you break up your AT work into two or more intervals, jog for at least 4 minutes between them. Increase the duration of the workout each time you repeat it. For example, your first AT run might be 2 × 10 minutes and your last one 2 × 20 minutes. Your pace will also gradually increase as you gain fitness. Shorten your recovery-week AT runs unless you feel great.

SI RUN: Between a warmup and a cooldown, do 8 to 12 intervals of 400m or 4 to 10 intervals of 400m plus 4 intervals of 200m, all at speed intensity. Jog 400m after each hard effort. Start with a workout duration that you can handle, and increase it as necessary over the ensuing weeks.

ENDURANCE RUN + OPTIONAL EASY X: Perform a high-aerobic-intensity run, 20 to 30 seconds per mile slower than marathon pace, that lasts at least 1 hour. If you wish, also do a shorter endurance cross-training recovery workout, with at least 4 hours of separation.

LI RUN: Run four to seven lactate intervals lasting 4 to 5 minutes each at aerobic-capacity intensity, with 3 to 4 minutes of active recovery between intervals. Start with a workout duration that you can handle, and increase it as necessary over the ensuing weeks.

MP RUN: Between a warmup and a cooldown, run the number of miles indicated at your goal marathon pace. Make sure to stay hydrated.

MI RUN: Do a mixed-intervals run of 200m to 400m speed intervals and 4-to-5-minute lactate intervals with appropriate recoveries. A shorter workout might be 2 × 400m, 2 × 1200m, 2 × 200m. A longer one might be 3 × 400, 3 × 1200, 3 × 400. Start with a workout duration that you can handle, and increase it as necessary over the ensuing weeks.

RACE PREP: In the morning, between a brief warmup and cooldown, complete a near-maximum effort lasting 150 seconds, recover for 3 minutes, and then sprint for 30 seconds. You may run, pool run, or ride a bike. Immediately after finishing this workout, consume 12 to 16 ounces of a sports or recovery drink. Maintain a carbohydrate-rich diet for the remainder of the day. This regimen will maximize glycogen storage in your liver and legs for the coming race.

RUNNER'S TRIATHLON PROGRAM

This 18-week program is designed to prepare runners for a first inter-
mediate-distance triathlon such as a standard Olympic-distance event
(1.5-K swim, 40-K bike, 10-K run). In this program, you will swim, bike,
and run two or three times per week and strength-train twice a week. I
have chosen not to identify key workouts in this schedule because nearly
every workout is of equal importance in a program such as this.

RUNNER'S TRIATHLON PROGRAM							
	DAY 1	**DAY 2**	**DAY 3**	**DAY 4**	**DAY 5**	**DAY 6**	**DAY 7**
Week 1 **Base 1**	Strength or off	SI swim	Easy ride	Easy run + strides or fartlek Strength	SI swim	Easy ride + jumps	Easy run + strides or fartlek
Week 2 **Base 2**	Strength or off	SI swim	Easy ride + jumps	Easy run + strides or fartlek Strength	SI swim	Easy ride	Easy run + strides or fartlek
Week 3 **Base 3**	Strength or off	SI swim	Easy ride + jumps	Easy run + strides or fartlek Strength	Easy ride + jumps	Bike brick LI swim	Long run
Week 4 **Base 4** **Recovery**	Strength or off	SI swim	Easy ride + jumps	Easy run + strides or fartlek Strength	LI swim	Easy ride	Easy run
Week 5 **Base 5**	Strength or off	SI swim	Easy run + strides or fartlek	Easy ride + jumps Strength	Fartlek	Run brick LI swim	Long ride
Week 6 **Base 6**	Strength or off	SI swim	Easy ride + jumps	Easy run + strides or fartlek Strength	Easy ride + jumps	Long run LI swim	Long ride
Week 7 **Build 1**	Strength or off	AT ride	SI swim	Speed run Strength	LI swim	Run brick	Long ride Long swim

RUNNER'S TRIATHLON PROGRAM (*cont.*)

	DAY 1	DAY 2	DAY 3	DAY 4	DAY 5	DAY 6	DAY 7
Week 8 **Build 2** **Recovery**	Strength or off	SI swim	AT run	LI swim	SH ride	Easy run Strength	Easy ride
Week 9 **Build 3**	Strength or off	AT ride	SI swim	Speed run	LI swim	Run brick Strength	Long ride
Week 10 **Build 4**	Strength or off	SI swim	AT run	LI swim Strength	SH ride	Long ride	Long run Long swim
Week 11 **Build 5** **Recovery**	Strength or off	Easy run + strides or fartlek	AT ride	SI swim Strength	Speed run	Easy ride	Easy run LI swim
Week 12 **Build 6**	Strength or off	AT run	SI swim	SH ride Strength	LI swim	Bike brick	Long run
Week 13 **Peak 1**	Strength or off	AT ride	SI swim	LI run Strength	LI swim	Run brick	Long ride
Week 14 **Peak 2** **Recovery**	Strength or off	AT run + strides	SI swim	AT ride	LI swim	Easy run Strength	Easy ride + jumps
Week 15 **Peak 3**	Strength or off	LI run + strides	SI swim	AT ride	LI swim	Run brick	Long ride + jumps Long swim
Week 16 **Peak 4**	Strength or off	AT ride	SI swim	AT run + strides Strength	LI swim	Long ride + jumps	Long run
Week 17 **Peak 5**	Strength or off	AT run + strides	SI swim	AT ride	LI swim	S/B/R brick	Easy ride + jumps
Week 18 **Peak 6** **Recovery**	Off	Easy run + strides or fartlek	SI swim	Easy ride + jumps	Race prep	Off	**Triathlon**

Workout Descriptions

STRENGTH OR OFF: Perform a 20-minute strength workout unless you need a day of complete rest. If you rest, be sure to perform a strength workout on one of the next 2 days so that you're consistently doing two strength workouts per week.

SI SWIM: After a thorough warmup and a drill set (see the recommended drill set in chapter 4), swim a set of short intervals (25, 50, 75, or 100 yards or a combination thereof). Swim at the fastest pace you can maintain through the complete set without form breakdown. Rest for 10 to 30 seconds between intervals. It's beneficial to go for lots of variety in terms of interval lengths and rest periods, as this approach stimulates consistent fitness gains. Start with a total of just 200 to 300 total yards of intervals if you are a relative beginner, and work your way up to as much as 800 to 1,000 yards toward the end of the cycle.

EASY RIDE: Perform an endurance-intensity ride of 40 minutes to 2 hours, depending on what your body is ready for.

EASY RIDE + JUMPS: Do an easy ride as described above, but in the middle portion, perform six 30-second efforts at 90 percent of maximum speed with full active recoveries.

EASY RUN: Perform a steady recovery- or moderate-aerobic-intensity run of 30 to 60 minutes, depending on what your body is ready for.

EASY RUN + STRIDES OR FARTLEK: Perform an easy run as described above, either followed by strides (four to six 100-yard speed runs separated by recovery jogs) or in the form of a fartlek, in which the easy pace is interrupted by six to ten 30-second bursts at speed intensity.

BIKE BRICK/RUN BRICK: A brick workout is a bike ride followed immediately by a run. Besides building endurance in both disciplines, this improves your ability to run in a fatigued state. All of the brick workouts in this training program should be performed in the moderate- to high-aerobic-intensity range. Each should emphasize either the bike or the run. In a bike brick, the cycling segment should be about four times the duration of the run segment. In a run brick, the run should last between 60 and 100 percent of the duration of the cycling segment. The duration of both types of brick workout should increase gradually throughout the training program until you reach an appropriate maximum duration, at which point they can level off (assuming the maximum is reached before your final recovery week). Your longest bike brick should be at least 90 minutes/25 minutes and need not exceed 3 hours/45 minutes. Your longest run brick should be at least 1 hour/45 minutes and need not exceed 90 minutes/80 minutes.

LONG RUN: Do a moderate- to high-aerobic-intensity run that lasts long enough to leave you moderately fatigued at the end. Your first long run should be about 10 percent longer than the longest easy run you have done recently. Gradually increase the duration of your long runs throughout the program until they reach an appropriate maximum duration, after which they can level off (assuming the maximum is reached before your final recovery week). Your longest run should be at least 70 minutes and need not exceed 2 hours.

LI SWIM: After a thorough warmup and a drill set, swim a set of long intervals (200, 300, or 400 yards or a combination thereof). Swim at the fastest pace you can maintain through the complete set without form breakdown. Rest for 30 to 60 seconds between efforts. As with your short interval swims, try to vary the long-swim workout structure from one workout to the next. Begin with a total of 400 to 600 yards of intervals, and work your way up to 800 to 1,600 yards.

FARTLEK: Run for 40 to 60 minutes at moderate aerobic intensity with a handful of speed-intensity bursts (20 to 60 seconds each) between chosen landmarks.

LONG RIDE: Do a moderate- to high-aerobic-intensity ride that lasts long enough to leave you moderately fatigued at the end. Your first long ride should be about 10 percent longer than the longest easy ride you have done recently. Gradually increase the duration of your long rides throughout the program until they reach an appropriate maximum duration, after which they can level off (assuming the maximum is reached before your final recovery week). Your longest ride should be at least 2 hours and need not exceed 4 hours.

LONG RUN + JUMPS: Do a long ride as described above, but do six to eight 20-second out-of-the-saddle sprints sprinkled throughout the ride.

AT RIDE/AT RUN: Between a warmup and a cooldown at recovery intensity, do between 12 and 40 minutes of anaerobic-threshold riding or running, but not more than 20 minutes consecutively. If you break up your AT work into two intervals, run or ride at recovery intensity for at least 4 minutes between them. Increase the duration of the workout each time you repeat it. For example, your first AT ride might be 2 × 10 minutes and your last one 2 × 20 minutes. Your pace will gradually increase as you gain fitness.

Speed run: Between a warmup and a cooldown, do 6 to 12 intervals of 400m or 4 to 10 intervals of 400m plus 4 intervals of 200m, all at speed intensity. Jog 400m after each hard effort. Start with a workout duration that you can handle, and increase it as necessary over the ensuing weeks.

Long swim: Swim for 25 to 45 minutes at a steady, moderate pace. Swim 25 minutes in your first long swim and gradually build up to 45 minutes.

SH ride: Between a warmup and a cooldown, bike 6 to 12 hill-climb intervals lasting about 90 seconds apiece with 2-to-3-minute active recoveries. Use a hill with a moderately steep grade of 6 to 8 percent. Perform the intervals at the fastest pace you can maintain through the end of the last interval. Feel free to make the workout longer as you gain fitness.

S/B/R brick: This is a triathlon dress rehearsal. Swim for 15 minutes, then immediately hop on the bike and ride for 50 minutes, and finally run for 30 minutes. Do each segment at a steady, comfortable pace.

Race prep: In the morning, between a brief warmup and cooldown on the bike, pedal for 150 seconds at maximum effort, recover for 3 minutes, and then sprint for 30 seconds. Immediately after finishing this workout, consume 12 to 16 ounces of a sports or recovery drink. Maintain a carbohydrate-rich diet for the remainder of the day. This regimen will maximize glycogen storage in your liver and legs for the coming race.

E I G H T

CROSS-RECOVERY

THERE IS NO SUCH WORD as *cross-recovery*. I made it up. It is meant to capture the notion that there is more than one way to recover from training besides simply not training, just as there is more than one form of training that runners should do in preparation for running events. The fact is that everything you do in your life affects your running: your other daily activities, your diet, your sleep, your thoughts and emotions, and any specific measures you take to promote recovery. Everything you do in your life affects your health, and the healthier you are, the better you will run.

In this chapter, I will talk about seven specific ways you can increase your overall health and promote recovery from training.

1. Creating synergy between running and other parts of your life

2. Optimizing nutrition habits

3. Maximizing sleep

4. Staying motivated

5. Managing stress

6. Getting massages

7. Treating injuries effectively

By doing these things, you will begin each workout (and race) with more energy, less soreness, and more motivation—and therefore you'll perform better.

CREATING SYNERGY BETWEEN RUNNING AND YOUR LIFE

While training for a half-marathon, a runner I was coaching developed a debilitating case of sciatica. It seemed unlikely that the running itself had caused it. He tried all of the obvious treatments that others and I recommended but got little relief. A student of Zen, he spent a lot of time meditating while sitting in a half-lotus position. On a hunch, he changed his sitting position, and sure enough, his injury healed very quickly thereafter.

This case history demonstrates just one of four general ways in which daily activities can affect one's training for the worse. In addition to increasing the body's susceptibility to injury, daily activities can drain more than their fair share of energy from the body, leave little time for training, and distract the mind from running, thereby sapping motivation.

Most of us spend the majority of our waking hours sitting at desks, in cars, and on sofas. So much sitting tends to result in muscular and postural imbalances—tight hip flexors and hamstrings, weak core muscles, and forward spine curvature—that can predispose runners to overuse injuries. Sitting properly will help you maintain good spinal posture and prevent the degeneration of your lower back and abdominal muscles. You should sit with your torso perfectly upright so that your spine is able to maintain its normal S curve. When sitting at a desk, use a chair that supports your back in this position, allows you to place your feet flat on the floor with a 90-degree bend in your knees, and allows you to sit very close to the desk so that you do not have to bend forward. Arrange your workspace in such a way that you can look straight ahead rather than having to look downward. In the car, in order to achieve good posture, you need to put the seatback in an upright position and hold the steering wheel low rather than high, and you will almost certainly have to place a small pillow or rolled towel behind the lumbar portion of your back, because most car seats are designed to accommodate deteriorated posture (a C-shaped curvature of the spine).

Even sitting with good posture is still sitting, so it tends to promote tightness and weakness in certain muscles. Sitting imbalances tend to limit running ability, and running tends to exacerbate certain sitting imbalances such as tight hamstrings. Functional strength training and flexibility training will counteract these effects.

The problems of energy and time drains are closely related. Many runners lack both the time and energy they would like to have for running for the same reason: They do too much in a day. Modern life is pursued at a frantic pace. Not everyone can swim against the stream of society, but with some clear prioritization and creativity, you can become at least an eddy in the stream—that is, still a part of things but going your own way. Here are just a few suggestions for finding a little more time and energy for running (all of which I have practiced successfully in my own life).

BE REALISTIC. Don't try to do too much. Back in high school, during a recruiting visit I made to Brown University, the cross-country coach told me, "Understand that if you come here, all you will do is study and run." He had a point. If you want to run well, running cannot be one of six or seven different "extracurricular" activities you pursue. Maybe the guitar lessons, the church volunteering, and whatever else can wait until after the marathon. If running is not that important to you—well, then, you can always keep the guitar teacher and forget the marathon!

RUN EARLIER IN THE DAY. Typically we have more energy available in the first half of the day than in the second half. If you're currently training after work and feeling sluggish, try running during your lunch hour or even first thing in the morning.

HIRE SOMEONE TO CLEAN YOUR HOME, MOW YOUR LAWN, WORK ON YOUR CAR, OR DO ALL OF THE ABOVE. Sometimes spending a little money really can solve problems—or reduce them, anyway.

PUT IN YOUR 40 HOURS (OR WHATEVER) AND NOT A MINUTE MORE. Many of us devote extra time to work not just because we are career-oriented but also out of fear—the fear that if we don't work overtime, we'll "look bad" in comparison to those who do. In my experience, runner-employees who insist on making time for training generally win even greater respect from their employers on account of their dedication to fitness and athletics—and, indeed, on account of showing "no fear."

TRAIN LIGHT DURING THE WEEK AND HEAVY ON THE WEEKEND. Triathletes routinely do 40 to 50 percent of their training on the weekends, and there's no reason runners cannot benefit from a similar schedule. You might, for example, do your hardest high-intensity workout on Saturday, your long run on Sunday, and a cross-training workout on each of these days, and then do as little as one key workout and two or three light workouts during the week.

BUY A TREADMILL OR INDOOR BIKE TRAINER. This will let you enjoy the convenience of working out at home sometimes.

ELIMINATE YOUR COMMUTE. Find a way to work from home (at least sometimes), move closer to your workplace, or change jobs. Many runners place an artificially low ceiling on the changes they can make to support their running, and I just don't get it. "Oh, I couldn't possibly pick up and move just to live close to those beautiful trails I like to run on!" Why not?

One other way to burn less energy during daily activities does not involve time: managing stress. The physiological stress response consumes a lot of energy. Most of us waste loads of energy by spending more time in a stressful state than we really need to. I'll talk more about stress and stress management later in the chapter.

Daily activities can also affect your running on a strictly psychological level by sapping your motivation to train. Just as your energy supply is limited, your daily capacity to psych yourself for hard work is also finite. When there is too much going on in your life, your motivation for one or more routine activities inevitably slides. Motivation is the psychological equivalent of physical recovery: Without either, it is impossible to train effectively, if at all. I'll share my favorite techniques for keeping motivation levels high in a later section of this chapter.

OPTIMAL NUTRITION HABITS

We generally think of training as being the sole determinant of our fitness gains. In fact, good nutrition is just as important as good training. Food provides the raw materials that training stimuli act upon to change your body for the fitter. Properly fueling your fitness gains is as simple as following seven basic nutrition guidelines.

1. EAT A BALANCE AND A VARIETY OF FOODS. The body needs a wide range of nutrients. No single food source contains more than a small fraction of this range. The basic food types you need to incorporate into most meals are whole grains, vegetables, fruits, nuts, legumes, and plant oils. If you eat animal foods, then meats, fish, eggs, and dairy products can round out your diet. The Healthy Eating Pyramid was developed by researchers at Harvard University to replace the outdated USDA Food Guide Pyramid. It shows the relative proportions of food types you should include in your diet. In addition to hitting each of these food types, you should eat a variety of foods within each type. For example, don't let broccoli be your only vegetable, as healthy as it is.

2. EAT MOSTLY WHOLE FOODS. Whole foods are foods that have been minimally processed from their natural state. They tend to be far more nutritionally dense than processed foods, many of which also contain unhealthy additives. Processed foods such as fried fast foods and snacks and packaged baked goods should have a very small place in your diet. They just waste space in your stomach.

3. REPLACE WHAT YOU BURN. It's normal to lose weight as you move from a low level of conditioning toward peak fitness. A runner who has been training consistently for a few months or more should maintain a consistent weight, which requires consuming a number of daily calories that is equal to the number of calories burned in a day. Instead

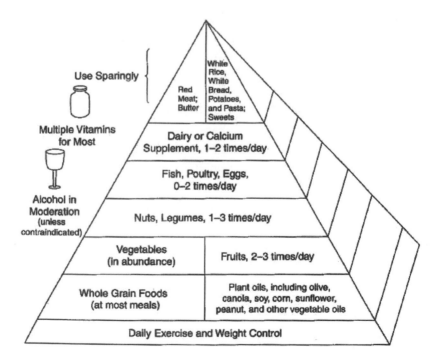

The Healthy Eating Pyramid

of counting calories, the easiest way to make sure you're consistently re-placing what you burn is to weigh yourself once a week.

You should also be sure to replace the three macronutrient types in the right proportions to offset losses. The typical endurance athlete burns and breaks down roughly 60 percent carbohydrate, 25 percent fat, and 15 percent protein and should therefore eat and drink in the same ratio.

4. EAT FOR SUSTAINED ENERGY. In order to have the energy you need for all of your daily activities plus your workouts, you need to eat fairly frequently throughout the day (for example, breakfast, morning snack, lunch, afternoon snack, dinner, evening snack) and to consume low-to-moderate-glycemic carbohydrates at each meal. The glycemic index is a measure of how quickly a given carbohydrate food is metabo-lized; the slower it's metabolized, the longer it provides energy.

A Penn State University study proved just how important carbohy-drate choices are with respect to energy yield. One group of athletes ate a rolled oats cereal (moderate-glycemic food) while another group ate a puffed rice cereal (high-glycemic) before a stationary cycling test. Both breakfasts contained 75 grams of carbohydrate. Those who ate the rolled oats cereal were able to cycle significantly longer than those who ate the puffed rice, due to greater glucose availability. In other words, those who had eaten the high-glycemic meal had used up more of the carbohydrate it contained before the workout even started.

5. STAY WELL-HYDRATED. Research suggests that many of us do not consume enough water and consequently live in a state of chronic mild dehydration. Adequate water intake is necessary for proper digestion, elimination of wastes, joint lubrication, and other essential functions. Poor hydration also compromises an athlete's performance by keeping blood volume below its optimal level.

Daily water needs are highly individual. They depend on factors in-cluding body weight, activity level (that is, training volume), other di-etary considerations such as alcohol intake (which increases water needs), and the weather. The *average* person requires roughly 1 ounce of water per kilogram of body weight on a daily basis. Athletes generally need a little more. There's no precise way to determine exactly how much water you need. It's best to simply carry a water bottle at all times and sip from it at regular intervals throughout the day.

During and immediately after exercise, water alone is not sufficient. During exercise, body fluid comprising both water and electrolyte minerals (sodium, chloride, magnesium, and potassium) is expelled from the body through sweating. As little as a 2 percent loss in body fluids will negatively impact cardiovascular performance. You can easily lose twice this amount during a hard workout.

Consuming a sports drink containing water and electrolytes is an effective way to limit fluid losses. However, during moderate-to-high-intensity exercise, it is not possible to restore water and electrolytes as quickly as they are lost. Even runners who are conscientious about hydration nearly always complete their workouts in a state of fluid deficit. This phenomenon is known as involuntary dehydration.

Runners routinely compound the problem of involuntary dehydration by failing to consume adequate quantities of water and electrolytes immediately following exercise. As a result, their blood volume stays low, which in turn slows the delivery of vital nutrients to the muscles and the removal of metabolic wastes from the muscles. The whole recovery process is thereby compromised. In order to ensure adequate restoration of water and electrolytes, in the first 2 hours after exercise, you should consume 1.5 ounces of water or a sports drink for each ounce of weight loss incurred during the exercise session. If you choose to drink water, be sure to supplement it with electrolyte-rich foods like fruits or vegetables.

The better sports drinks have been formulated not only for optimal hydration but also for optimal carbohydrate delivery. Carbohydrate is the primary fuel that powers the muscles during moderate-to-high-intensity exercise. The body cannot store it in quantities great enough to fuel intense efforts for extended periods of time, so you should consume carbs during workouts lasting 60 minutes or longer and also during all high-intensity workouts. Many studies have shown that by consuming easily digested forms of carbohydrate in a fast-absorbing solution during exercise, endurance athletes can perform at a higher level for longer periods of time.

Many sports drinks contain carbs such as sucrose and glucose in a 6 to 8 percent concentration, which is the maximum concentration that the average athlete can absorb during hard exercise without experiencing gastrointestinal problems. These drinks are by far the best way to get carbohydrate while running. Alternatives such as fruit juices and sodas have too many of the wrong kinds of carbohydrates. The only alternatives to sports drinks that I can recommend are carbohydrate gels, which must be consumed with water.

A few of the newer sports drinks contain, in addition to electrolytes and carbohydrate, a small amount of protein or amino acids. Research shows that in the right ratio and concentration, a combination of carbohydrate and protein delays fatigue even more than a conventional sports drink and also significantly reduces muscle tissue damage.

6. TAKE ADVANTAGE OF THE MUSCLE-RECOVERY WINDOW. What you eat and drink in the first 2 hours after a workout is just as important as what you do in the workout itself. It is during this so-called acute-recovery period that your body makes its physical adaptations to the training stimulus. Consistently taking in the right nutrients in the right amounts during this muscle-recovery window will help you to recover faster, adapt more fully, and eventually wind up far ahead of those who do not take advantage of the window.

A study performed at a Canadian university showed just how great a difference recovery nutrition can make even in the short term. A group of 10 female endurance athletes on a controlled diet were fed a postexercise snack of either a carbohydrate-rich energy drink or a placebo drink that tasted the same but had no energy value. On the days when subjects received the placebo, they were given the energy drink at breakfast so that their total caloric intake for the day was always the same. The study found that the athletes were able to exercise 47 percent longer, on average, in a ride to exhaustion the day after they received the postexercise energy drink. This illustrates that postworkout energy consumption is critical for accelerating recovery and preparing the body for the next workout.

The nutrients you most need after exercise are the same ones you need during exercise: water, electrolytes, carbohydrate, and protein. We've already discussed the importance of postworkout fluid replacement. Immediate postexercise carbohydrate and protein intake is even more important, because during the first hour after exercise, the muscle cells are much more receptive to insulin, the hormone responsible for transporting amino acids and glucose. Thus the body can synthesize glycogen (the storage form of carbohydrate) and build muscle proteins two to three times as fast during the first hour or so after exercise than it can at other times—as long as it is provided with the raw materials. As a general guideline, try to consume 10 to 20 percent of your daily carbohydrate intake in the first 1 to 2 hours after a workout. For every 4 grams of carbohydrate, also consume about 1 gram of protein.

Many runners find it most convenient to get their postexercise nutrition by continuing to drink the same carbohydrate-protein sports drink they used during the workout, because it's often much easier to drink than to eat a full meal soon after exercise.

7. SUPPLEMENT WISELY. The typical healthy runner who eats right probably does not need any of the scores of available nutritional supplements. Even a daily multivitamin is not a necessity, though if you don't consume the full complement of vitamins and minerals in your diet on a given day, a vitamin can fill in the gaps. Be careful not to abuse this form of dietary insurance. There are hundreds of healthy phytonutrients (plant nutrients, most of which are still unnamed and unknown) that you will never find in any vitamin pill. Besides which, there's growing evidence that vitamins, minerals, and phytonutrients work best when delivered in the proper balance—specifically, the very balance in which they are found in real foods.

Some supplements can be effective as treatments for specific disorders or health risks. The only nutritional deficiency that is at all common in runners is anemia, or iron deficiency. It is hypothesized that impact forces destroy hemoglobin, the iron-rich oxygen transporter in blood. Because women typically consume less iron than men and lose blood through menstruation, they are more susceptible to exercise-related anemia, although low blood-iron levels are fairly common in male runners, too. The primary symptom of anemia is persistent fatigue. If you are suffering from ongoing lethargy that has no obvious cause, have your iron level checked at your next doctor's visit. If it's low, the problem can be corrected through a period of rest and increased iron intake. The recommended daily intake of iron for athletes is 10 to 20 milligrams.

Glucosamine and chondroitin sulfate are natural compounds that the body uses as building blocks for a variety of soft tissues, including joint cartilage. Some research has shown that supplementation with glucosamine and chondroitin sulfate can counteract the pain and immobility associated with osteoarthritis and prevent or reverse cartilage breakdown. With this in mind, many runners take a glucosamine or combined glucosamine/chondroitin sulfate supplement in hopes of preventing or treating the cartilage damage that is sometimes caused by the long-term repetitive shock of running. To date, no study has investigated the prophylactic use of such supplements by athletes, but scientists will very likely pursue this line of research before long. In the meantime, based on what we know about these supplements today, I think that taking a glucosamine/chondroitin supplement is not a bad idea.

MAXIMIZING SLEEP

Sleep is as fundamental a need as food. Long-term deprivation of either will kill you, and even small inadequacies can cause harm. Any factor that compromises health also compromises athletic performance, and sleep is no exception. Insufficient sleep reduces the body's ability to process glucose and therefore to produce energy. It also heightens levels of cortisol, a stress hormone that attacks muscle tissue and therefore must be suppressed in order for proper postworkout tissue repair to occur. In addition, human growth hormone, the muscle-building hormone that plays the biggest role in rebuilding tissue after exercise, requires sleep for full activation, so the less sleep you get, the less muscle you wake up with. Sleep loss also weakens the immune system by reducing the activity of interleukins, molecules involved in signaling between cells of the immune system.

While individual sleep needs can vary widely, the well-known 8-hour standard seems to be about right for most adults. Athletes often need slightly more sleep than nonathletes. Sleep experts believe that a majority of adults in our society are chronically sleep-deprived. According to the latest surveys, the average American adult now sleeps less than 7 hours a night during the workweek. Such night-in, night-out deprivation will take the edge off your performance, at the very least, and could lead to greater health issues over time.

Here are some tips you can use to ensure you get enough sleep.

KEEP A SLEEP LOG. For a week or two, record how much sleep (hours and minutes) you get during each 24-hour period. Determine the average amount of sleep you get per night and also how much you get on weekends or holidays when you are able to wake up when you feel like it. This second figure represents the amount of sleep you need each night and therefore the amount you should try to get every night.

ANALYZE YOUR SCHEDULE. Which evening activities cause you to go to bed late? Which morning routines cause you to wake up early? Look for ways you can rearrange your schedule so that you can go to bed earlier, wake up later, or both. Cutting down on evening television viewing is one way to get to bed earlier. Making tomorrow's lunch and laying out your work clothes in the evening can streamline your morning routine and allow you another 20 minutes in the sack.

NAP IF POSSIBLE. If you can fit a 20-minute catnap into your day, do it. The first minutes of sleep are the most beneficial, so 20 minutes is almost as good as a couple of hours.

CUT DOWN ON DIETARY STIMULANTS. To combat the fatigue caused by chronic sleep deprivation, many of us fall into nutrition habits that produce a short-lived artificial wakefulness by overstimulating the nervous and endocrine systems. Excessive consumption of caffeine, sugar, and alcohol is common among the sleep-deprived. This pattern only makes matters worse by causing the nervous and endocrine systems to grow dependent on nutritional stimulation for "wakefulness," with the result that your quality of sleep becomes even worse. Limit yourself to one cup of coffee in the morning and one to two alcoholic beverages a day. Drink water instead of soda or fruit juice throughout the day.

GO TO BED AND WAKE UP AT MORE OR LESS THE SAME TIME EVERY DAY, EVEN ON WEEKENDS. This will train your body to fall asleep easily at the appropriate time and sleep soundly the whole night through.

CREATE A SLEEP-PROMOTING ENVIRONMENT. You will fall asleep faster and sleep more soundly if your mattress and sleeping position are comfortable and your room is very dark, quiet, and cool. Sources of white noise, such as electric fans and fountains, also tend to induce sleep.

DEVELOP A BEDTIME ROUTINE. The last hour of your day should be conducted in a way that prepares your body for sleep. Read a book, listen to quiet music, meditate, or take a bath.

STAYING MOTIVATED

You cannot have too much motivation to run. Motivation is simply desire. The greater your desire to run, the more consistent you will be in your training, the more effort you will put into your training, and the more you will enjoy running. As an ultimate result, you will achieve greater fitness gains and better race performances.

Because you cannot have too much motivation to run, you should actively cultivate it. Individual runners are motivated in different ways. Some are motivated primarily by time goals, others by age-group competition, others by the camaraderie of training with a group. Much as the process of finding an optimal training approach requires that you treat yourself as an experiment of one and pay careful attention to the ways your body responds to various training stimuli, the process of achieving optimal motivation requires that you study the influences that increase and decrease your motivation. For example, if you find that you enjoy running on trails far more than on roads, go out of your way to run on trails.

All runners, however well they understand their motivations, experience the occasional day or week of low motivation. This is perfectly natural and nothing to get alarmed about. In such situations, it is best to have a bag of motivational tricks that you can draw upon for help in overcoming the training blahs. Here are a few such tricks.

CROSS-TRAIN. As I mentioned in the first chapter of this book, one of the many benefits of cross-training is that it introduces more variety into training and thereby helps to keep motivation levels high. Just because you feel unmotivated to run on a given day does not necessarily mean you feel unmotivated to exercise. If you would rather swim, then swim!

MODIFY YOUR RUN WORKOUT. Sometimes you're just not motivated to perform the specific run workout you have scheduled for the day. In these cases, replacing the scheduled workout with another type of workout can provide a quick motivational boost. If you were going to run from home, drive to the beach and run; if you were going to run long and slow, run shorter and faster; or whatever.

Usually, we think of workout modifications as being necessitated by physical factors, but it's sometimes appropriate to modify workouts for the sake of motivation. Such adjustments are better than the all-or-nothing approach wherein the scheduled workout is either suffered through or blown off altogether.

CHANGE YOUR GOAL. For many runners who compete in races, event goals are the biggest motivators. Often, when such runners lose motivation, it is because the event goal they are currently pursuing fails to excite them or because an event goal is lacking altogether. Renewing your motivation in such instances can be as easy as reconsidering your next big goal and coming up with something that feels exciting.

FIND A PARTNER OR A GROUP. Good company can be a motivational boost. On a day of low motivation, you might be able to overcome it with a well-timed invitation from a fellow runner. Investigate the possibility of finding an organized group to train with a couple of times a week or more.

GET MORE FEEDBACK. Evidence of progress is another powerful motivator. Increasing the amount of performance feedback you receive can therefore cure the training blahs. You might, for example, begin using a computer to graph your results in key workouts, wearing a heart rate monitor during workouts, or measuring your body composition (body fat percentage) periodically.

BUY SOMETHING. There is a child still in each of us. I have yet to meet the runner who is too "mature" to get charged up by purchasing a snazzy new running outfit. Of course, unless you're very rich, you cannot motivate yourself in this manner every day. For that matter, even if money is no object, the novelty of doing each run in a snazzy new outfit will wear thin. But the occasional well-timed purchase of shorts, shoes, socks, sunglasses, a watch, or whatever can exploit the kid inside you for a motivational boost.

TAKE A BREAK. Sometimes the best way—perhaps the only way—to respond to low motivation is to lay off training for a while. Nearly every runner needs the occasional mental break from the discipline and hard work of training. Even the professionals take breaks. Don't allow fear of losing fitness to prevent your taking a break when you need one. Yes, you will lose fitness, but it comes back as quickly as it fades, and your renewed enthusiasm for training will more than make up the difference in the long run (so to speak). Most runners feel the hunger begin to return after as little as 2 to 3 weeks away from formal training. In any case, wait for that hunger to return before you return to hard training.

STRESS MANAGEMENT

Stress is a physiological response to physical and mental stimuli that threaten your well-being in one way or another. These stimuli can range from anxiety about a work deadline to an extremely hard workout. The stress response is characterized by increased blood pressure, changes in neural activity (increasing activity in the fear centers of the brain), the release of energy-releasing hormones such as adrenaline (which prepare you for "fight or flight"), and other alterations in body state. This physiological response evolved thousands of years ago, when threats tended to be more extreme (rampaging saber-toothed tigers and so forth) but also a lot less frequent. It is an effective means of dealing with genuine threats; however, when triggered too often, the stress response itself is harmful. The problem is that our bodies were not designed to switch into stress mode several times every day, yet that's exactly what they do in this frantic-paced modern world, and it's not good for our health or our athletic pursuits.

Chronic stress is associated with a long list of symptoms, some of which can be life-threatening over the long term. High blood pressure, ulcers, gastrointestinal disorders, insomnia, back pain, and sexual dysfunction are all on the list. Even before it leads to major medical problems, though, stress is bad enough. Besides being rather unpleasant to experience, it wastes a lot of energy, leaving you with less fuel to perform well in the office, on the roads, and everywhere else.

It's important to make a conscious effort to manage stress in your life. Here are a few ways to do so.

IDENTIFY AND MANAGE KEY STRESSORS. Most of us are set off repeatedly by the same stressors day after day: our bosses, other relationships, our commutes, public speaking, even low self-esteem. Try to step outside yourself and learn about the stimuli that set you off. This awareness will let you condition yourself not to react reflexively to these stressors.

TAKE TIME OUT FOR FUN. Every day you should do something that you enjoy, purely for the satisfaction of it. The experience of enjoyment directly counteracts the effects of stress. Laughter is particularly effective in this regard. University studies have shown that laughter can significantly reduce physiological markers of stress. So be sure to frequently read funny books, watch funny movies or TV programs, hang out with funny people, and use your own sense of humor at home and at work.

CULTIVATE A PEACEFUL ENVIRONMENT. You can experience a great deal more relaxation during the day by cultivating more peaceful environments in the places where you spend a lot of time—home and office, for most of us. Furnish and decorate in an uncluttered fashion, keep your surroundings clean and tidy, listen to gentle music, add more light, introduce pleasant aromas through potpourri or an aromatherapy lamp, keep fresh flowers and potted plants, or even get a pet.

PRACTICE RITUAL RELAXATION. Meditation and breathing exercises have been proven to lower stress levels in clinical experiments. Just a few minutes of such an activity per day can make a big difference.

Here's a simple breathing exercise you can try. Lie down comfortably on your back with your head on a pillow. Close your eyes, relax all of your muscles, and begin breathing slowly, deeply, and evenly, inhaling through your nose and exhaling through your mouth. Gently push all thoughts out of your head, and focus your full attention on feeling and listening to your breath.

Bear in mind that running and cross-training can be either stress relievers or stressors. Reduced stress and a greater capacity to handle stress are among the adaptations that result from consistent exercise. Every runner is familiar with the experience of feeling frazzled before a run and relaxed afterward. Even hard workouts do more good than harm when performed as components of a sensible training program.

But exercise can increase stress levels when it becomes yet another demand on a body and mind that are already overwhelmed by the rest of the day's activities. For this reason, it's important to arrange your lifestyle in such a way that your running and your other daily activities accommodate one another.

MASSAGE

Massage seems to aid recovery in a variety of ways. I say "seems to" because scientists have so far been mostly unable to prove that massage has the beneficial effects that athletes believe it has. Of course, it is not at all unusual for athletes to be a step ahead of scientists. Athletes can feel what works and what does not; what other proof do we need? Nowadays, the feeling that massage does indeed work is so strong and universal that nearly all elite runners receive weekly or even daily massage treatments—and a rapidly growing number of dedicated amateurs are following suit.

Massage works first of all by elevating circulation and thereby accelerating the delivery of nutrients to the muscles and the clearing of metabolic wastes from the muscles. It also loosens tight spots in the muscles, known as trigger points, and breaks up scar tissue, thus increasing freedom of motion and often reducing pain and preventing injuries. A good massage therapist can also help you prevent injuries less directly by discovering muscle imbalances that you can then work to correct, through stretching and strength training, before they lead to breakdown. Some experts believe that massage therapy may also enhance the efficiency of motor signaling.

Individual massage therapists differ from one another in terms of style, area of expertise, and ability. Your best bet is to find one who specializes in sports massage, has years of experience, and comes highly recommended. You can get recommendations from fellow runners or by quizzing a local running coach. If you can't get a recommendation, just use a phone directory and ask a few questions of any massage therapist before committing to an appointment. Some questions include: How long have you been practicing? How many of your clients are runners? What sort of formal training and certifications do you have? While there is no single "gold standard" certification for a sports massage therapist, the answer you receive to this third question should establish that the therapist you're quizzing has received rigorous and broad training.

Expect to pay in the range of $45 to $65 an hour for massage. If you cannot afford a full hour every week, do a half hour every week or a full hour every other week.

Between trips to the massage therapist, you should also self-massage. Every other day or so, rub some massage oil into your legs, and knead the muscles by applying deep pressure with your thumbs and sliding them downward (away from your heart) a few inches at a time. This technique works well for the calves, shins, quadriceps, and hip flexors.

In order to get at your hamstrings, hips, and groin, you will need the help of a self-massage device such as the Stick, which functions somewhat like a rolling pin on the muscles. Many running specialty shops carry such tools. The Stick goes for about $25.

In chapter 3, I described three stretchlike therapeutic exercises utilizing a foam roller that might also be described as self-massage techniques. The spine mobilization exercise restores mobility to the vertebrae; the iliotibial band massage counteracts the tightening of the IT band that nearly all runners experience; and the buttock trigger-point release reduces pain in and restores mobility to the piriformis muscles deep inside the buttocks.

PAIN AND INJURY TREATMENT

Too often runners try to ignore or work through pain, and the results are usually disastrous. Whenever you experience pain during or after a workout, you should address it immediately and aggressively. Begin the treatment process with step one in the following six-step protocol. Sometimes step one will take care of it. If not, move on to step two, and so forth.

1. DISCONTINUE THE PRESENT WORKOUT. Never try to train through anything more than very mild discomfort that does not increase as the workout proceeds. Use your judgment. If you see a red flag coming from your knee or hip or whichever part of your body hurts, stop immediately and walk home if you have to. Abandoning a workout is certainly frustrating, and it takes a good deal of restraint for a dedicated runner to do it. But when you are able to exercise such restraint, you will seldom miss more than 1 or 2 days of training. On the other hand, if you try to push through pain, your body will break down to the point where you have no choice but to lose whole weeks of training. As Ben Franklin said, a stitch in time saves nine.

2. REDUCE INFLAMMATION. Tissue inflammation accompanies all overuse injuries. In fact, the pain you feel when an overuse condition develops is generally caused less by the injury itself than by inflammation that develops as the body tries to heal itself. While treating the symptoms of pain and inflammation alone solves nothing, it is a very helpful measure to take in conjunction with efforts to deal with the underlying problem.

The preferred treatment for inflammation is to frequently ice your sore areas. Cover the skin with a towel or other protective layer, then apply ice for 20 minutes at a time, removing it for 10-minute periods between applications. Combining a cold treatment with compression of the sore muscle—for example, with a neoprene sleeve—is even more effective. Elevating the affected area may also reduce swelling and the associated pain.

Use an anti-inflammatory medication such as ibuprofen (Motrin or Advil) only occasionally, in cases of extreme discomfort. Long-term dependence on such medications may result in damage to the liver and kidneys and reduce your body's ability to handle inflammation on its own. Try not to stay on them for more than 2 weeks at a time. When soreness borders on the intolerable, first try using a topical anti-inflammatory sports cream, such as Flex-Power. And always bear in mind that no medication accelerates muscle healing and that training hard with lingering muscle damage—even if the pain is covered up—will only cause further damage.

3. MODIFY YOUR TRAINING. The main reason runners try to train through injuries is that they fear the loss of fitness that will result if they stop running. But training does not have to be all or nothing. In most cases, you can maintain your fitness level despite an injury and without compromising healing by modifying your training appropriately. When you develop an overuse injury that does not allow you to train normally, quickly figure out what sorts of training you are able to do, and move into a modified program that is as close to your normal program as you can make it without hindering healing and rehabilitation. Although you might not be able to do any road running at all, you still might be able to ride a bike or run in water. Shin splints are an example of an injury that might prevent you from doing any running.

With other injuries, you might still be able to run but not as you normally would. For example, with a relatively mild case of plantar fasciitis, you might be able to run on a treadmill rather than on roads. With a relatively mild hamstrings strain, you might be able to run slowly but not quickly. And with a relatively mild case of compartment syndrome (swelling inside one of the muscles on the front of the lower leg), you might be able to run short distances but not far.

Even when an injury forces you to abstain from all cardiovascular exercise involving the lower extremities, there's almost always something you can do: physical-therapy stretches and strengthening exercises, swimming without kicking, and so on.

4. DIAGNOSE THE PROBLEM. Waste no time in determining the precise nature of your injury. While the specific diagnosis has little bearing on the initial steps taken in response to overuse pain (you'll want to modify your training and treat the inflammation no matter what), finding out what's wrong is vital in treating the underlying cause and making sure the injury never recurs. Even if the affected area responds quickly to the initial treatments, you'll want to investigate the cause.

There are nine common overuse injuries in runners. The lion's share of running injuries belongs to one of these nine types, which makes diagnosing injuries easy, as long as you know the symptoms. The table on the opposite page lists these injuries along with their primary symptoms and most frequent causes, as well as helpful treatments and recommended cross-training activities you can do in place of running while you rehabilitate. It is safest, however, to consult a medical professional. There's always the chance that your injury is not what you think it is, and you can waste a lot of time treating and rehabilitating a misdiagnosed injury. A second reason to seek a medical professional for diagnosis is that a single injury can have different causes or combinations of causes in different runners. A good orthopedist, podiatrist, or physical therapist is far better able than the average runner to accurately identify the causes of a specific injury in a particular runner and is therefore more likely to prescribe the right treatment and rehabilitation program.

COMMON RUNNING INJURIES

NAME OF INJURY	SYMPTOMS	FREQUENT CAUSES	TREATMENTS	CROSS-TRAINING
Piriformis Syndrome	Pain and tightness in the buttock	Shortening of piriformis muscle through overuse, frequent sitting, faulty biomechanics	Stretching, massage	Any pain-free endurance activity except cycling
Iliotibial Band Syndrome	Pain just beneath the hip bone or just above the knee on the outside of the leg	Overuse, weak hip abductors	Stretching, massage	Any pain-free endurance activity
Hamstrings Strain	Pain in the hamstrings, usually near the buttock or the knee joint	Tight hamstrings	Ice, anti-inflammatories, gentle stretching	Any pain-free endurance activity
Patellafemoral Pain (Runner's Knee)	Pain in and around the knee joint during running	Overpronation, weak hip abductors	Orthotics, motion control shoes, relative rest	Any pain-free endurance activity
Shin Splints	Pain on medial side of shin, usually in dominant leg	Too much too soon	Relative rest, ice	Any non-weight-bearing activity
Stress Fracture	Concentrated area of pain, usually in the lower leg or foot	Repetitive impact	Relative rest	Any non-weight-bearing activity
Achilles Tendinitis	Pain and swelling in the Achilles tendon when running	Tight calves, weak ankle flexors, overpronation	Ice, anti-inflammatories, orthotics, motion control shoes, gentle stretching	Any pain-free endurance activity
Plantar Fasciitis	Pain in the heel when running and upon rising from bed in the morning	Tight calves, overpronation	Orthotics, motion control shoes, night splinting	Any non-weight-bearing activity
Compartment Syndrome	Pain in the shin after several minutes/miles of running	Too much too soon, individual anatomy	Stretching, massage, ice, anti-inflammatories, relative rest	Any pain-free endurance activity

Further, your specific injury might require treatments that you cannot perform on your own, such as ultrasound.

Be sure that the expert you consult specializes in treating runners or other athletes. The typical medical professional who does not understand running tells every injured runner to take 2 weeks off. Heeding this prescription may cause you to lose fitness needlessly and then develop the same injury once you return to training because you have done nothing to address the root cause.

5. MANAGE THE PROBLEM. Injury management devices can in some cases allow you to continue running even as you rehabilitate the injury. Patellar knee straps redistribute impact forces and allow some runners suffering from patellafemoral pain syndrome to run with little or no discomfort and without exacerbating the condition. Most running specialty stores carry these straps, which cost $15 to $20. Heel and ankle taping often allows runners with plantar fasciitis to run without heel pain. Consult a physical therapist to learn proper taping procedure. Shoe inserts can prevent overpronation and thereby manage any one of the several types of running injury that overpronation can cause. These, too, are available at most running specialty stores. Most cost between $20 and $40. Just keep in mind that managing an injury is not the same as correcting its cause.

6. CORRECT THE CAUSE. Most overuse injuries in runners are caused by a combination of muscular imbalances and doing too much too soon. To permanently cure such injuries, you need to correct the particular imbalances associated with them. Sometimes the main culprit may be obvious. For example, if you have extremely tight hamstrings and you develop a hamstrings strain, there is little guesswork to be done. Often, however, the proximate cause of an injury is not the only causal factor. In the musculoskeletal system, everything is connected, so it is not rare for imbalances on one side of the body to cause injuries on the other or for imbalances up high to cause injuries down low.

This suggests two courses of action. One is to work with a sports massage therapist, physical therapist, or doctor capable of identifying all of the imbalances that have contributed to your injury. The second is to maintain a consistent and comprehensive program of strength training and flexibility training that will address any and all imbalances you may have. This is something I recommend that all runners do regardless of the nature of their injuries and even if they are healthy. If you want to train hard and injury-free, cross-training for injury prevention is essential.

SAMPLE TRAINING LOG

Week Beginning: ___

Goals: ___

Monday A.M.

Fatigue: _____

Soreness: _____

Workout: Running / Endurance XC / Stretching / Strengthening

Workout Description: _____

_____

_____

_____

Notes: _____

_____

_____

Monday P.M.

Fatigue: _____

Soreness: _____

Workout: Running / Endurance XC / Stretching / Strengthening

Workout Description: _____

_____

_____

_____

Notes: _____

_____

_____

Tuesday A.M.

Fatigue: _____

Soreness: _____

Workout: Running / Endurance XC / Stretching / Strengthening

Workout Description: _____

_____

_____

_____

Notes: _____

_____

_____

Tuesday P.M.

Fatigue: _____

Soreness: _____

Workout: Running / Endurance XC / Stretching / Strengthening

Workout Description: _____

_____

_____

_____

Notes: _____

_____

_____

Wednesday A.M.

Fatigue: _____

Soreness: _____

Workout: Running / Endurance XC / Stretching / Strengthening

Workout Description: _____

_____

_____

_____

Notes: _____

_____

_____

Wednesday P.M.

Fatigue: _____

Soreness: _____

Workout: Running / Endurance XC / Stretching / Strengthening

Workout Description: _____

_____

_____

_____

Notes: _____

_____

_____

Thursday A.M.

Fatigue: _____

Soreness: _____

Workout: Running / Endurance XC / Stretching / Strengthening

Workout Description: _____

_____

_____

_____

Notes: _____

_____

Thursday P.M.

Fatigue: _____

Soreness: _____

Workout: Running / Endurance XC / Stretching / Strengthening

Workout Description: _____

_____

_____

_____

Notes: _____

_____

_____

Friday A.M.

Fatigue: _____

Soreness: _____

Workout: Running / Endurance XC / Stretching / Strengthening

Workout Description: _____

_____

_____

_____

Notes: _____

_____

_____

Friday P.M.

Fatigue: _____

Soreness: _____

Workout: Running / Endurance XC / Stretching / Strengthening

Workout Description: _____

_____

_____

_____

Notes: _____

_____

_____

Saturday A.M.

Fatigue: _____

Soreness: _____

Workout: Running / Endurance XC / Stretching / Strengthening

Workout Description: _____

_____

_____

_____

Notes: _____

_____

_____

Saturday P.M.

Fatigue: _____

Soreness: _____

Workout: Running / Endurance XC / Stretching / Strengthening

Workout Description: _____

_____

_____

_____

Notes: _____

_____

Sunday A.M.

Fatigue: _____

Soreness: _____

Workout: Running / Endurance XC / Stretching / Strengthening

Workout Description: _____

_____

_____

_____

Notes: _____

_____

_____

Sunday P.M.

Fatigue: _____

Soreness: _____

Workout: Running / Endurance XC / Stretching / Strengthening

Workout Description: _____

_____

_____

_____

Notes: _____

_____

_____

Week's Totals

Running: _____

Endurance XC: _____

Stretching: _____

Strengthening: _____

Week Beginning: ___

Goals: ___

Monday A.M.

Fatigue: _____

Soreness: _____

Workout: Running / Endurance XC / Stretching / Strengthening

Workout Description: _____

_____

_____

_____

Notes: _____

_____

_____

Monday P.M.

Fatigue: _____

Soreness: _____

Workout: Running / Endurance XC / Stretching / Strengthening

Workout Description: _____

_____

_____

_____

Notes: _____

_____

_____

Tuesday A.M.

Fatigue: _____

Soreness: _____

Workout: Running / Endurance XC / Stretching / Strengthening

Workout Description: _____

_____

_____

_____

Notes: _____

_____

_____

Tuesday P.M.

Fatigue: _____

Soreness: _____

Workout: Running / Endurance XC / Stretching / Strengthening

Workout Description: _____

_____

_____

_____

Notes: _____

_____

_____

Wednesday A.M.

Fatigue: _____

Soreness: _____

Workout: Running / Endurance XC / Stretching / Strengthening

Workout Description: _____

_____

_____

_____

Notes: _____

_____

_____

Wednesday P.M.

Fatigue: _____

Soreness: _____

Workout: Running / Endurance XC / Stretching / Strengthening

Workout Description: _____

_____

_____

_____

Notes: _____

_____

_____

Thursday A.M.

Fatigue: _____

Soreness: _____

Workout: Running / Endurance XC / Stretching / Strengthening

Workout Description: _____

_____

_____

_____

Notes: _____

_____

_____

Thursday P.M.

Fatigue: _____

Soreness: _____

Workout: Running / Endurance XC / Stretching / Strengthening

Workout Description: _____

_____

_____

_____

Notes: _____

_____

_____

Friday A.M.

Fatigue: _____

Soreness: _____

Workout: Running / Endurance XC / Stretching / Strengthening

Workout Description: _____

_____

_____

_____

Notes: _____

_____

_____

Friday P.M.

Fatigue: _____

Soreness: _____

Workout: Running / Endurance XC / Stretching / Strengthening

Workout Description: _____

_____

_____

Notes: _____

_____

_____

Saturday A.M.

Fatigue: _____

Soreness: _____

Workout: Running / Endurance XC / Stretching / Strengthening

Workout Description: _____

_____

_____

_____

Notes: _____

_____

_____

Saturday P.M.

Fatigue: _____

Soreness: _____

Workout: Running / Endurance XC / Stretching / Strengthening

Workout Description: _____

_____

_____

_____

Notes: _____

_____

_____

Sunday A.M.

Fatigue: _____

Soreness: _____

Workout: Running / Endurance XC / Stretching / Strengthening

Workout Description: _____

_____

_____

_____

Notes: _____

_____

_____

Sunday P.M.

Fatigue: _____

Soreness: _____

Workout: Running / Endurance XC / Stretching / Strengthening

Workout Description: _____

_____

_____

_____

Notes: _____

_____

_____

Week's Totals

Running: _____

Endurance XC: _____

Stretching: _____

Strengthening: _____

INDEX

Boldface page references indicate photographs or illustrations.
Underscored references indicate boxed text.

Minerals, 211
Moderate aerobic running,
    146–47
Modification, of training, 219–20
Montgomery, Carol, **187**, <u>187</u>
Motivation
    as cross-recovery step, 213–15
    enhancing, 16, 214
    maintaining, 213–15
    running faster, 8
Mountain bike, 124–25
Movements
    bending, 37
    lunging, 37
    pushing and pulling, 37
    of running stride, 37–38
    strength training and, 37–38
    twisting, 37
Multivitamins, 211
Muscle-recovery window, 210
Muscles. *See also* <u>specific types</u>
    abdominal, **28**, 30, 37
    Achilles tendon, **29**, 31
    balance of, 27, **28**, **29**, 30–33, 30,
        31
    dorsiflexor, 27, 31
    fascia, **31**, 32
    force-producing, 27
    gastrocnemius, 27, **29**, 31, 72
    gluteal, **29**
    hamstring, 27, **29**, 32, 66, 72
    hip abductor, 27, **30**, 32, 72
    hip adductor muscles, **28**, 72
    hip flexor, **28**, 72
    iliotibia band, **30**, 32
    imbalances in, 2, 4–5
    oblique, **30**, 37
    plantar flexor, 27, 31–32, 37
    pulled, 71
    quadricep, 27, **28**, 72
    soleus, 27, **29**, 31, 72
    spinal erector, **29**, 30, 37
    stabilizing, 27, 30
    strain, 32

tibialis anterior, 27, **28**
trapezius, **29**

N

Napping, 212–13
Nutrition, 206–11

O

Oblique muscles, **30**, 37
O'Brien, Cathy, **67**, <u>67</u>
Off-season phase, 16, 215
O'Sullivan, Sonia, **22**, <u>22</u>
Overend, Ned, **21**, <u>21</u>
Overload, progressive, 152–53
Overpronation, 31–32, 36, 139
Overuse injuries, 2, 4–5, 32, 220

P

Pace at given intensity level,
    <u>150–51</u>
Partners, running, 214
Passive flexibility training, 66,
    68, 74
Patellafemoral pain syndrome,
    32
Peak phase of training cycle,
    163
Peak race, choosing, 160–61
Perceived effort, 146
Performance, running, 3
Phytonutrients, 211
Plan-and-adjust approach to
    training, 157–60, 174–75
Plantar fasciitis, 32
Plantar flexion strength-training
    exercises
    Standing Calf Raise, 39, **39**
    Straight-Leg Hop, 41, **41**
    Supine Bridge Heel Raise, 40, **40**
Plantar flexor muscles, 27, 31–32,
    37